LETTERS TO
Girls Who Dream
OF FLYING

Shona O.L. Bramble

DEDICATION

For my late great-grandmother, Jestina "TanJes" Creese, who had very little but never held herself nor her family back from taking flight. May she continue to fly in the Beautiful Beyond!

CONTENTS

ACKNOWLEDGMENTS

To the women in this book - this book would not be a reality without you. Thank you for being so generous and for being so open in sharing your stories, your fears, your accomplishments and your dreams. I would like to thank each and every one of you from the bottom of my heart. Without your words, without your honesty and your openness, this book would not be complete. You are all very special to me and you have all overcome in different areas of your lives – I pray that you continue to overcome difficulties and challenges and find peace in every aspect of your lives. Thank you for trusting me with your truth. May you each continue to live the lives you dream of in a world that sometimes isn't kind or fair to any of us. Continue to take flight and soar!

To my family who have always been supportive of my efforts and have been supportive of this book, I appreciate your support and your love. My love to all of you – always!

To my special friends and mentors who have guided me and supported me in the moments when I wasn't so sure of myself. You held me up in the moments I was questioning my own abilities. Thank you for sticking by my side and providing me with encouragement and love.

PROLOGUE

One day in 2014, I sat in my living room crying, as I had been for several days. I felt sorry for myself—I was depressed, sad and defeated. I was entering my ninth week of unemployment, my just-six-month-old relationship had come to an end, and I was in the middle of a health crisis.

I didn't know what to do, and I didn't know how to soothe myself. I didn't have the energy to create; my love for photography had dwindled and I did not feel like writing. Somehow, I knew that this was temporary, but I wondered when it would end. When would I feel like my old self again?

As I wiped my tears, a news story on the television grabbed my attention. It was about a domestic violence case. My sadness turned to anger because I couldn't fathom how this could happen. Sure, I'd heard stories like this before—although I was never a victim of domestic abuse, I knew other people who had been. But my body shook as I thought of the victim in this story.

I started to wonder, *How could this be? Why has she decided to stay? Why is she allowing this?* But I was at a loss for answers to my own questions. I wanted to talk to her, tell her that everything would be okay, and tell her that if I could have hope for a better life even though it was falling apart, she could too.

I wondered, *If I could write her, what would I tell her? Or what would I tell other girls who were in her shoes?* I wondered if by writing letters to girls, I could help at least one person see the light and get help. *Could I help a woman, a young girl, pursue her dream of flying, even soaring to her highest potential?*

But my idea seemed incomplete. So I thought about my wise and thoughtful friends who had also experienced challenges in their lives. I wondered if they would be willing to share their stories too. What would they say to someone who is fearful of chasing her dream and needs to find hope?

Then the idea for this book came to me.

I contacted around 40 women whom I have known in some capacity in my life. They all represented as many diverse backgrounds as possible. I asked them a series of questions, assuring them that they could express themselves as freely as they wanted.

In asking the questions, I was curious to know how these women were affected by dreams that did not take flight. I wanted to know how they coped with personal issues. I was also curious about how their self-perception differed from how others perceived them because I believe that when we have a different perspective from how others see us, it can hold us back. I was curious to know what their passions were and what kept them moving forward. Finally, I wanted these women to go back in time and speak to their younger selves so that they could compare how they see themselves now with how they saw their former selves.

This book contains their responses—their letters—on how they were able to face fears and challenges and fly in a way that works for them. None of these women are bulletproof from life's injustices, but they have all found a way to persevere. They have had the strength to write about their experiences, even though it may have been difficult, in order to help someone they don't know.

Many of the letters have similar responses and themes, but I think it's perhaps because we are more alike than we are different. While the themes establish a commonality, the individual responses make these women unique and special in their own way.

But most importantly, I wanted these women's stories to help you understand that it's okay to not have it all figured out, and that it's okay to have not lived the exact dream that you've dreamt. As long as you are living an authentic life and working towards the greater good, you are already complete.

FLIGHT 1: THE BARGAINERS

The women in this chapter whom I have identified as bargainers are women in the corporate world. They remind me of two successful businesswomen I knew when I was growing up. My cousin owned a small grocery store and bar while raising her children, and there was also a woman who owned a classy, high-end boutique in the city, which was something you didn't see very often.

It was nice to know the persons behind the business powerhouses—they were strong and funny, and one was a master at hosting the simplest of dinners.

If your dream is to take flight as a bargainer, the women in this chapter have a few things they would like to share with you on how they took flight.

"If you can't fly then run, if you can't run then walk, if you can't walk then crawl, but whatever you do, you have to keep moving forward.
-Dr. Martin Luther King, Jr.

Dear Beautiful,

My name is Rachel and I'm in my 40s. I was born in St. Vincent and the Grenadines, but now I live and work in Antigua.

When I was growing up, I wanted to be a lawyer or a teacher. Today, I am the general manager of a five-star hotel. My special gifts are connecting with people—making others feel comfortable by being able to put myself in others' shoes.

I am passionate about my daughter, living a full life, dancing, mentoring young women, and helping those less fortunate. When I am doing the things I am passionate about, I feel alive and grateful. My daughter brings me the most joy; she has brought me to a place of grace and gratefulness. Being with her reminds me that faith can move mountains, and it humbles me.

When I mentor young girls and when I dance, I feel alive! I feel like I don't have to make any effort. The peace I feel in these moments is effortless, and I am immeasurably happy. If I couldn't do these things, I would definitely feel that something was missing. I would feel spiritually dead and empty.

The things that I feared most when I was growing up were rejection and poverty. They were my fears as a child, a teenager, and a young woman. But now I no longer have those fears, and they have made me passionate about caring deeply for others. I am always making sure that my actions don't make others feel rejected, and I'm always working towards improving the lives of those less fortunate. My fears became the catalyst for the things I am now passionate about.

If I could go back and speak to my younger self, I would tell her, "Be brave. Be yourself. Love yourself. Don't dim your light so that someone else's could appear brighter. You are perfect and wonderfully made, and the things that you feel insecure about are the same things that are going to propel you to being a successful mother, wife and businesswoman. Laugh, laugh hard, and laugh some more!"

I think one of my biggest challenges has been finding my voice in a male-dominated world—at least that was the case at the beginning of my career. Balancing work and family life has also been a challenge.

But working hard and being professional at all times have assisted greatly in getting my voice heard. The balancing act between family and career requires time management skills, and I have set rules that do not allow me to compromise my family commitments. I have also been blessed with an understanding and supportive husband who helps out a great deal. When things get difficult, I also have a supportive family and some strong sister-friends that I met along my journey. After getting my 'pray on', I turn to the wisdom of the incredible women in my life—my moms, sisters and sister-friends.

So how do I hold myself back? Even now I have to remind myself that it's okay for me to shine, that it's okay for me to take the stage, but that it's also okay to hold back. To push myself forward, I look at the examples of women who inspire me. I also constantly remind myself of various mantras. One of my favorites is, "The height which great men reached and kept were not attained by sudden flight. But they, while their companions slept, were toiling upwards in the night." I recited this poem at age five; the head of my school gave it to me to learn and recite, and it has stayed with me all my life. It's my go-to mantra when I want to push forward.

I see myself as a caring and sincere person. I feel that others see me as strong and bold. Self-acceptance is an ongoing process for me; I have to always remind myself that I am enough. The things that I value most in life are my family, peace, joy and loyalty.

Beautiful, I believe your biggest struggle is self-acceptance. I believe we live in a superficial society, so we buy into all of the hype of the media with their stereotypical ideas of beauty.

If I had the opportunity to sit with a young girl who is a shadow of my younger self, my words to her about her dreams would be, "Be bold. Be yourself. You are enough—more than enough. Love yourself. Don't spend a whole lot of time trying to explain to others who you are. You are special and unique. You need not dim your light for anyone or any reason. Shine! Be! Most of all, be grateful."

- Rachel

Dear Beautiful,

My name is Sofia and I am in my 40s. I was born in Puerto Rico, but I now live in the United States of America.

When I was growing up, I wanted to be a flight attendant. Today, I am a regulatory compliance officer. I believe that I have creative gifts when it comes to scrapbooking and card-making. I am a loyal and great friend, and a loving mother and wife.

I am passionate about my family, my friends and my new home. When I am doing the things I am passionate about, I am over the moon! If I couldn't do those things I would be incredibly sad and incomplete.

The things I feared most growing up were being unhappy and alone. Now, I feel that those fears were part of my life's journey; sometimes, you need to find yourself first and find out what you really want. This is a long process, and some people might not get there. I'm glad I did.

If I could go back and speak to my younger self, I would tell her, "In time, you will find all the answers to your questions, but the journey is as important. Oh, and invest in Google!"

One of my biggest challenges has been being in the workforce. I work on combatting that challenge daily. The banking world is a man's world, and I feel like I have to compete with the Boys' Club every day. When it comes to career opportunities and compensation, the disparities are evident, but I am not giving up.

When things get difficult, especially at work, I rely on my amazing crew, as we call ourselves. We help each other with work-related issues, and we also vent to each other and provide feedback. It's a great way to release stress and the negative energy that sometimes builds up.

I sometimes hold myself back because I can be negative, I put myself down, and I doubt my abilities. Yes, I am insecure, but I get great affirmation from my peers.

In order to push myself forward I try to stay motivated by keeping myself current; it helps a lot in my line of work because laws and regulations change constantly.

I see myself as an average person. I feel that others see me as more than average. The things I value most are my family and friends.

Beautiful, I feel that that your biggest struggles are self-image and weight-related issues. What I feel contributes most to your struggles are the media, especially reality television.

If I had the opportunity to sit with a young girl who is a shadow of my younger self and talk to her about her dreams, I would tell her,

"Your dreams will all come true, just maybe not in the way you imagine them and not at the time you want. But when you are ready, they will just happen."

- Sofia

Dear Beautiful,

My name is Kerry and I am in my 40s. I was born in St. Vincent and the Grenadines, but today live in Canada.

When I was growing up, I wanted to be a teacher. Today, I am an assessment analyst.

I definitely feel like I have special gifts. I have a way of connecting and motivating people. I am passionate about helping others and when I am doing the things I am passionate about, I feel a joy in my soul. If I couldn't do the things I am passionate about, I think I would feel complete sadness.

As a child, the thing I feared most was meeting new people. But now, I enjoy interacting with new people. If I could speak to my younger self, I would say, "You have the power and strength to speak up for what you believe and want."

One of the biggest challenges I face is that people underestimate my ability. But in order to combat that feeling, I keep pushing forward to do my tasks with pride, and that allows me to exceed expectations.

When things get difficult for me, I speak with my siblings or I pray. Sometimes, I feel like I hold back on my capabilities because I don't

want others to feel that I want to outshine them. In order to push myself forward, I read motivational and inspirational writings.

I see myself as someone who is intelligent, loyal, caring and successful. I feel like others see me as intelligent, loyal, caring and assertive. To work on self-acceptance, I remind myself that I am blessed, favored and unique. What I value most in life is my relationship with my family and friends.

Beautiful, I believe that your biggest struggle is living up to other people's ideas of the body sizes and types needed to be successful or famous. I think that the media, television and magazines all contribute to your struggle.

If I could have a moment in time to sit with a shadow of my younger self, I would tell her, "Dreams should be what you are passionate about, and they should motivate you each day. Don't live your life based on others' achievements or their physical attributes. You are special, smart, and can succeed in life if you discipline yourself to do the things that will allow you to be in the best position to accomplish your goals."

- Kerry

Dear Beautiful,

My name is Tikeetha and I am in my 40s. I was born in the United States, where I reside today.

When I was growing up I wanted to be a dentist. I'm not sure why, but I think it was because I had such a fascination with teeth! I wanted to make sure that everyone had beautiful teeth and beautiful smiles. However, life didn't work out as I planned. I realized in college that I needed to study chemistry in order to be a dentist, and I hated chemistry.

So, I'm not a dentist. I work in Human Resources as a benefits analyst. I analyze plan designs, make recommendations for benefit changes, analyze the company's expenses and revenues, and write requests for proposals. I'm the jack-of-all-trades for my team, and I'm truly happy.

My special gift is my attitude. It is what I'm most proud of. Early on, I realized that my attitude determines my altitude. I could either soar high above the clouds, believing in the possibilities and understanding that the situation I found myself in was temporary, or I could hold on to the pain, animosity and anger, and let life defeat me. But I chose to soar. Some days are better than others, but my attitude is one of gratitude, and I'm thankful for all the experiences because they are teachable moments.

My passion is writing. I've always been a writer. Ever since I was a young girl, I would journal my thoughts or poems in a book. I didn't realize it at the time, but journaling helped me keep my thoughts clear when the world seemed like it was raging in my head. It was at the end of my marriage that I got back to what I knew and loved.

When I'm writing, I'm creating a roadmap of my life or situation. Its details are hammered out in pen or on the computer, and they allow me to review the situation and see if I can find a different perspective or outcome.

If I couldn't write I would probably go crazy, both literally and figuratively. I need to get my message out by any means necessary. I'm often seen in meetings writing notes that have nothing to do with my job but everything to do with my passion. I'm always thinking of storylines or book ideas. I blog, so I'm constantly thinking of topics or issues that I want to share with my readers. Blogging is my therapy, and again, I would go crazy if I couldn't write.

I feared for my safety when I was a teenager. I was molested, raped and sexually assaulted all before the age of 14. I felt alone. I felt unlovable. I was a beautiful girl who never dressed inappropriately, but it didn't matter. I couldn't control what happened to me. I had to learn that it wasn't my fault.

I'm not afraid anymore. Through therapy and my faith, I've overcome that fear. I learned that I did nothing wrong. That knowledge encouraged me to feel comfortable in my own skin. I'm now an advocate for change. I understand what it is like when you don't feel beautiful and you think the world around you is looking at you, but the reality is that all will be as it should.

If I could go back and speak to my younger self I would say, "This too shall pass." I think that was one of the lessons I struggled with as a teen and young adult. When something bad happened, I thought it was the worst thing that ever happened to me. I couldn't imagine that anything in life could be more painful than what I was experiencing at that time. But my grandmother used to say to me, beloved, "Trouble don't last always." You will have good days and bad days, but I promise you that it will get better and this situation you find yourself in will pass.

One of the biggest challenges I face is being a woman of color in corporate America. I walk a fine line of trying to fit into the culture and still being taken seriously. I have to battle many stereotypes. Professionalism is the key, along with staying true to who I am. I've attended meetings where I felt completely disrespected, yet I kept my composure and addressed the issues clearly and calmly. I didn't yell, scream or raise my voice in outrage and disgust (which might have been appropriate), but I remembered that I got into my position based on my knowledge and skills, and because I was the most qualified. Don't take your anger out in the workplace, and understand that you will have some good bosses and some bad bosses, but you are there to do a job. So, do the job well, Beautiful!

I started a relationship with God at a young age. I had a praying grandmother and a praying mother. I learned from my mother that sometimes parents wish that they could kiss every tear that falls from their child's eyes and make things better for them. However, when you can't "fix it no more," you need to get on your knees and pray. Give it to God! He will hear and He answers prayers. My help comes from God.

I think I hold myself back by doubting or second-guessing my skills. I spend so much time trying to be twice as good as other men and women that when the light shines on me, I shy away from the spotlight and wonder if the compliments are genuine. Yeah, they are! I need to acknowledge the compliments, thank the giver and keep pushing forward.

Speaking of pushing forward, one of the things that I do to push forward is to constantly reassess my goals. I have goals set for three months, six months, nine months, one year and three years. This helps me to keep adjusting and striving for something. Whether it is a vacation, paying off bills or looking for a promotion, it helps to visualize and strive for your goals.

I see myself as a feminist. Feminism is simply advocating for the rights of women. Women deserve to be treated equally in all things— socially, politically and economically. As I tell my son, "Anything a boy can do, a girl can do. We are equals." Don't let people tell you that you can't be something you want to be, and don't allow people to pay you a lesser wage than a man if you do the same job. We have to fight for our rights, not just in the workplace, but socially and politically as well. We have to make sure that we are not being ignored. As Beyoncé sings, "Girls run the world!" Now that you've taken up your flag and you're ready to march for the equality of women, some people may see you as being different.

I see myself as different. Different is good. Don't ever think that you have to fit in. You were born to stand out. I know when I say that I'm a feminist that some people think that I hate men. That is the furthest thing from the truth. I love men. I'm raising a son. But, I don't think people should allow women to be treated as second-class citizens. We hold some of the highest positions in this country, such as Supreme Court judge or U.S. Attorney General. We've come far, but there is still much to do.

I am a firm believer in speaking life over your situation. Constantly tell yourself that you are beautiful, smart, funny or nerdy. Speak your truths. Own them and love them. You have to embrace everything about you. We were all individually and wonderfully made. I have a weirdly shaped nose and thick thighs, and it took me a long time to love and accept the person that I am. Every day when I wake up and go about my routine, I look in the mirror and encourage myself.

More than anything in this world, I value time. Time spent and time wasted. Every minute counts. Some people didn't wake up this morning, but valuing the time you have on Earth allows you to keep things in perspective and make the most out of each day and each moment. The seconds become minutes that become hours that become a day. Each day matters. Time matters. Don't waste your time on unhealthy situations or unhealthy people. Appreciate all that you have and all that you don't because there is a lesson in the shortage.

Beautiful, I think one of the biggest struggles you face today is the need for self-exploitation. You are constantly being told that you don't matter unless you have a huge number of followers on Twitter or Instagram. You believe that you matter not by the words of wisdom you utter, but the need to stoop to peer pressure. You don't owe anyone anything. Being famous for not having a talent is an unrealistic goal. We need to change our mindset and understand that it is the content of our character that matters.

I think the media and many of us adults contribute to your struggle. We watch the videos on WorldStar Hip-Hop, YouTube and Facebook. We engage in the foolishness of reality television and try to tell you that it is just fun, but we are "robbing Peter to pay Paul" by living a lifestyle above our means. We are making you think that a big butt, fake lashes and lots of designer clothes make you important. But it doesn't. It makes us victims of consumerism.

Your dreams matter, Beautiful. They do. Nothing is impossible. When people look at my life and say, "You're so accomplished," I respond, "There's no difference between the next person and me; I just wanted it more." That's it. Want it more. Dream in color and make sure that you know that you can achieve anything you set your mind to. You will have successes and you will have failures, but the most important thing to do is to keep believing that you can do it.

- *Tikeetha*

FLIGHT 2: THE EDUCATORS

Education is a very important part of my life. My passion for sharing knowledge is something that I have always embraced, and as an adult, I've shared knowledge through mentorship. For many of us, education gives us freedom.

When people ask me why I migrated to the United States, I tell them that one of the biggest reasons was to have the opportunity for an education I may not have gotten had I stayed in my island home. Coming to the United States allowed my family many opportunities, and we have used them rightly and justly. So this chapter includes letters from women who are educators, who have spent their life tending to minds, making sure that their students' brain matter stays sharp so that we all can fly high.

"Education is not the filling of a pail, but the lighting of a fire."
-William Butler Yates

Dear Beautiful,

My name is Annis and I am in my 60s. I was born on the island of St. Vincent and now live in the United States.

When I was growing up, I wanted to be a nurse. Today, I am a teacher. I believe that I have been blessed with the gift of being able to genuinely advise and inspire others.

My main passion in life is to see my granddaughter succeed in high school and go to college so that she can have a decent and successful life. My other passion is to be able to complete one or two more years of teaching before retiring so that I can do other things, such as write my story, or possibly write short stories about the life experiences of different people.

I used to be very passionate about teaching, but over the years, students have begun to want to know less of what I would like them to learn. As a result, I had to reduce my content. Later on, I observed that their interests were waning, and they preferred to listen to music or hide their mobile devices in their laps to watch videos during class.

However, I intend to keep my passion for seeing my granddaughter succeed. I hope that after I retire, I'll be able to put my energy into writing and doing other hobbies that can also potentially earn me income. If, for some reason, I could not fulfill some of these things, I would feel that it is the will of God. When things don't work out, I feel that God knows best. This is because I usually think carefully about what I plan to do.

As a young woman I was plagued with many fears, and they intensified because I was physically and psychologically abused as a child, a teenager and a young woman. One of my biggest fears was the whipping I would receive from my aunt if I did not do my chores on time or if I forgot to do them.

Looking back, I realize that those fears adversely affected me for a very long time. I do not think that I have overcome the negative effects of what I experienced. The most I do now is to not think of my aunt because any time I do, tears come to my eyes. The reality is that when you are a child, you look to the significant adult in your life to care for you. Any time that this is not done, indelible scars remain. As adults, we try to put the bad treatment we received behind us. If we talk about the past, everything comes to the foreground. As I get older, I realize that people like my aunt had their own problems and took them out on people like me.

Sometime after I turned 40, I was able to tell my younger self that I was not the problem, but it was my aunt who had many problems and many fears. Since she was not able to solve her own problems, she was transferring them to me.

My biggest challenge has been getting my daughter to follow my advice. I combat that challenge with prayer. Humility plays a great part in keeping my sanity.

When things get difficult, I talk to good friends, my mother and God. Some friends may not be able to advise or help, but at least when you talk about things, it helps you to exhale and inhale, to think again about the problem. At times I rest or sleep, and later I get a new perspective.

Sometimes, holding yourself back may seem like a physical act, but it may be a spiritual act. For example, I am qualified to be an educational administrator, but I have never applied for that job. When my colleagues ask why I haven't, I say that I felt like my family situation did not allow me to pursue that path. Another deterrent is that I will never drive far from my home. Therefore, I am content to remain a classroom teacher.

In terms of pushing myself forward, I am at the end of my career. I went back to school and obtained a master's degree in education administration, and I am constantly attending staff development sessions. Although the topics are not entirely new, they wear new labels.

I see myself as successful and wise. I feel that people also see me as successful and wise. Even people of my age look to me for advice. Self-acceptance is an important aspect. A long time ago, I believed that my face was for identification only. So physically, I dealt with my face first. Sometimes I would tell a student, "Let's exchange—I'll take your face and you take my face." It's a way to tell them that they are beautiful while at the same time validating them as we share some humor.

I value integrity, honesty, truth, love, and caring for self and others. God is in control.

Beautiful, I believe your biggest struggle is that you may come from a dysfunctional home. Some of you are separated from your parents. Some of you are abused, and some of you have mental problems.

If I had the opportunity to sit with a young girl who is a shadow of my younger self, I would tell her a bit about my background. I wouldn't detail my abusive past because sometimes young people cannot comprehend the depth of my commitment, and might even mock my situation. However, I would encourage that young girl to talk to her guidance counselor for advice on her educational path. I would advise her to explore and research the path toward college. I would advise her about the need to focus on her education and to make a plan.

- *Annis*

Dear Beautiful,

My name is Ms. B. and I am in my 70s. I was born in Jamaica but I live in the United States.

When I was growing up, I wanted to be a teacher. Today I am a teacher.

I am passionate about teaching academics and life lessons, keeping healthy, and enjoying family and friends. How do I feel? First and foremost, I feel so blessed! I am gratified that I have touched so many lives for the better. If I could not do these things, I would feel deprived, and I would strongly envy those who could.

Growing up, what I feared most was not being accepted by others. Today I feel that there are some qualities I have that are liked by some, however people are not obligated to like all of me. Whatever traits I have that are liked, I put them out there and hope someone can benefit from seeing them in me.

If I could go back and speak to my younger self I would say, "Girl, you are beautiful, physically and spiritually. You can achieve anything you want to be. Yes, you can be a teacher and change lives for the better. You can take people from the unknown to the known. What a great contribution you will make to the world. Go for it!"

One of my biggest challenges in life was adjusting to a new country while raising a daughter singlehandedly. In order to combat challenges in my life, I try to set realistic goals and establish an alliance with a source outside of myself—God.

When in need of help, I seek help first from God, and then my professional mentors and supportive family members. But to be honest, it has been just God and me because I am such a private person.

I have held myself back by not making wise financial decisions earlier in life and not taking enough risks. I tend to procrastinate and play it safe. In order to push myself forward, I talk with successful and positive people who emulate what I can live within my means.

I see myself as a stable, independent and successful woman with a lot to achieve. I feel that different people see me differently, but many see me as a professionally successful woman—one who is independent, loves people, and is blessed with the gift of speech.

In order to work on self-acceptance, I try to be my true self, I accept people for who they are, share my values, and respect those of others. What I value most in life are education, my family, true friends and good health.

Beautiful, I think part of your struggle is identifying who you are and who you want to be in the future. What contributes to this struggle is the world we live in, mixed values, and a lack of guidance.

If I had the opportunity to speak to a shadow of myself, I would tell her to dream realistically and big, to work hard, focus, take it one day at a time, and ask for healthy advice.

- Ms. B.

Dear Beautiful,

My name is Leanne and I am in my 40s. I was born in Guyana and I live in the United States.

When I was growing up, I wanted to be a pediatrician because I loved babies. And then I wanted to be a fashion designer, not because I felt I knew the right fashions, but rather because I felt like I had a particular style that I wanted to share, and because some of my earliest memories were of watching my mother sewing. Today, I am a teacher by profession, and I am currently a stay-at-home mom.

I'm a creative thinker and I'm good with my hands. I am passionate about books, the idea that parents are their children's first teachers, the idea that all children need two parents, and the knowledge that humans are unstoppable if they survive childhood knowing they are beautiful, smart and powerful beyond measure.

When I am doing the things I am passionate about, I am most alive, while time and the distracting need for anything—food, comfort, or what my living reality tells me I should be doing or thinking instead—seem to be suspended in time. If I couldn't do those things, I would feel dead inside, like my reality was like a theater of the absurd play.

As a child, the only thing I feared were things that I thought could potentially change my life and tear my family apart—Guyana's war with Venezuela, and an uncle hurt by someone else. As a teenager, I feared getting pregnant or disappointing my mother in some life-changing way. As a young woman, I was afraid of living a dull and boring life without the diversity of people, cultures, ideas or places.

So how do I feel about those fears now? They are still true. But now I know that I am much more in control of my life—if not over what happens, then definitely to the extent to which I allow those fears to form a filter for how I view my life and control my life's path.

If I could go back and speak to my younger self, I would tell her, "Stop worrying and live life like you're stranded in the ocean but want to live. Relax; don't tense up and fight the water. Instead, work with it and it'll take you where you want to go."

My biggest challenge has been finding the courage to pursue dreams on my own without the support and encouragement of those around me. In order to combat this challenge, I talk to myself, coaxing myself to be strong. I tell myself not to give up on my dreams— never accept that they'll always be deferred or unrealized.

When things get difficult, I talk to my mom often, and I turn to God always. I feel like I hold myself back in spending too much time thinking about what I should be doing, instead of actually doing it. I also feel like I don't have enough drive to be satisfied with making baby steps without any gratification that I'm headed in the right direction.

In order to push myself forward, I keep my dreams alive and stay curious and open to what the world has to offer in people, ideas and experiences. I see myself as a work in progress—happier and more contented than I think am (I know I don't fully enjoy the present because I'm always thinking about the future in some part of my head).

I don't know and don't truly care to know how others see me because I know that how I see myself is most important. I see myself as someone who is kind to others, humble, works on having a relationship with God, and treats others the way I want to be treated. Working on self-acceptance for me is to focus on my strengths—

change the things I can, accept the things I cannot change, and hope God gives me the wisdom to know the difference. What I value most in my life are my kids, my husband, my family, and the personal contribution I make to the world.

Beautiful, I sense that your biggest struggle is believing that what you tell yourself and know on the inside is more important than all the messages you get from the outside world. What I believe contributes to that struggle is your easy willingness to accept what society tells you is true or good or is worth valuing.

If by some chance I had the opportunity to sit with a young girl who is a shadow of my younger self, I would tell her, "Quincy Jones once said, 'Dream really big dreams, bigger than what you think you can actually accomplish, and just have an ounce of faith that it's possible.' Lastly, know that the universe will rise up to make it come true."

- Leanne

Dear Beautiful,

My name is Lori and I am in my 40s. I was born in the United States where I currently reside.

When I was growing up, I wanted to be a ballerina, a missionary and a marine biologist. Today, I am a linguist and a scientist-in-progress.

My special gifts include solving puzzles and understanding how things work. I am passionate about people being treated with dignity and about making the world a better place. I feel like I have finally found my home when I am doing the things I am passionate about. If I couldn't exercise my passions, I would feel like part of my soul had been amputated.

My greatest fear from early childhood to early adulthood was of becoming my mother. Now that I am a mature adult, I am grateful that my mother was a non-traditional role model, and she always emphasized the value of education. Now I can accept and relish the traits we have in common, such as a sense of adventure, a need for regular self-expression through the arts, and the pioneering spirit to cut one's own path through the wilderness, as opposed to following the well-worn road that everybody else follows.

If I could speak to my younger self, I would say to her, "Speak up about what you like and don't like, especially with your family. Don't be afraid to take some control over, and responsibility for, your own choices. Like everything else in life, if you don't practice self-determination, you'll never get any better."

One of my biggest challenges has been low self-esteem, which has made me doubt my worth and own instincts in all aspects of life, and has often led me to settle for less than I deserved or needed. In those rare instances where I was nevertheless able to make more assertive choices, my negative self-concept still hampered me by significantly delaying the completion of my goals. In other words, I lost a lot of time getting to whatever the next step should have been, which in the end also reduced the sum total of my choices over a lifetime.

Now, at present, I know that if I can't motivate myself, I need to ask for help from a trustworthy, inspirational source. When things get difficult for me, I seek help from one of my closest confidants and friends. I also talk to my parents a lot, and sometimes even my sister.

I hold myself back in that I tend to be overcautious with people, especially at work. This is basically the flip side of not trusting my own intuition, experience and knowledge. But what helps me to push myself forward is being social with the people whom I find nurturing and inspiring. Also, I know it's important to build 'restorative niches' (see *Quiet*, by Susan Cain) every day, which for me could be reading a good book, going for a walk outside, doing yoga, having a power nap (with sensory deprivation), etc.

I see myself as intelligent, hardworking and loyal. I feel like others see me as eccentric and occasionally flighty. Writing in my journal and working on my worthwhile relationships with trusted friends, family and health professionals, have been ways in which I work on self-acceptance. What I value most in life are the opportunities I've had, in particular through education and travel.

Beautiful, your struggles are very real. Our whole culture is biased towards sexualizing you way too early, which is a basic control tactic. It starts as early as kindergarten, with negative body comments and less valued speech, with almost all our cultural cues working together to herd your psyche into a corral of sorts, where you can be easily branded and sorted.

What continues to add to these struggles is that there is no true equality yet in the United States, and every piece of the cultural puzzle assembled teaches girls and women that they will be less powerful, less valued, and less physically safe than their male peers.

If I had a moment, an opportunity where I could sit with a young girl who is a shadow of my younger self, I would say, "Trust your dreams and instincts. These are some of the saddest casualties of growing up as a woman today, yet trusting your dreams will be a more reliable guiding light if you can find the inner—and outer—resources to trust yourself. It's your life. You only get one lifetime, and there is no dress rehearsal. Only you can make your life as fulfilling, satisfying and rewarding as you need or want it to be."

- Lori

FLIGHT 3: THE HEALERS

As a young child growing up in the Caribbean, one of the first healers I knew was my grandmother, Iona Bramble. I recalled her leaving very early in the morning and never returning until night. Then there were the times when she worked on night duty, and she had to sleep at the geriatric hospital where she worked, taking care of those who were wounded, not just physically, but mentally and otherwise. Her story, her letter, is in this chapter.

Taking care of our physical selves and mental selves is so vital to our existence, and I appreciate those who spend exorbitant amounts of time serving the sick. The healers, as I call them in this chapter, have helped to heal either broken bones or minds, and so we honor their work, their spirit and their contribution.

"The practice of forgiveness is our most important contribution to the healing of the world."
- Marianne Williamson

Dear Beautiful,

My name is Iona and I am in my 80s. I was born in St. Vincent and the Grenadines, but I now live in the United States.

When I was growing up, I didn't know what I wanted to be because I did not have the time to think of anything. Life was difficult and I had to find work at a young age. However, as luck would have it, I ended up being a geriatric nurse for more nearly 40 years. Today, I am retired and enjoying my life.

God has given me the gift of looking after those who are helpless and are in need. Helping others is something that I've always been passionate about. When I was working and doing that which I was passionate about, I felt great. I am also passionate about prayer, and so I pray for families and for the world, leaving all things to God.

When I was a young woman, I was fearful about a lot. I tried to be brave because the area where I grew up was tough for a young person. I often traveled alone and at night. My safety was the thing I was most fearful about. Fast-forward to my current life, and I am no longer afraid. I believe that prayer has helped me to get past those fears.

If I could go speak to my younger self, I would tell her to be brave. I would tell her to not to be so sad. I would tell her that it will be okay eventually. Growing up in the times that I did, my biggest challenge was not being able to go to school and having to be a caregiver in my early life. There was not much I could do to combat those challenges until I found God.

I worked very hard. Back then, life was hard, and I had to develop an appreciation for what I was doing because there were not many opportunities. Once I found the Bible, that's where I found solace. When things got difficult for me, then and now, I seek God and trust Him for everything. He will take care of everything in His own time.

At this time of my life, at 80-plus years old, there's not much to hold me back; I am happy with my life and I have achieved all that I can achieve. In order to push myself forward back then, I had to turn my head away from the difficulties and think of how much better things would be. I accepted the blessings of those who I took care of and nurtured.

The way I see myself now is as someone who did all she could do in life. I tried to make myself happy in spite of difficulties, and I prayed daily to our creator to keep me. I am happy now, but it has not always been like that.

I feel that others see me as a loving person. They continuously bless me. Now that I'm older, I know that my family is doing the best they can to make sure I'm taken care of. They see me as a survivor. I recall old friends on seeing them—they would welcome me with open arms, great love and respect. People show me love, which makes me happy, and that's all I could ever hope for.

I believe I have achieved self-acceptance because with a good heart and a good mind, I know I've tried to do the best in life. I have asked God and myself what more I could have done, and when I do, I feel like I've done the best I could.

I value God first, and then my family—I trust that God will take care of them. I always try my best to be there for family. I never left them and will never leave them.

Beautiful, I feel that there is so much you struggle with—it's immeasurable. Life for you may even be harder than in my time, when I was in my prime. I believe that you must use your head in order to make the best choices in life. The thing that I see as the biggest struggle today for you is that you may want to live the fast life. No one wants to slow down and just be patient and wait.

If I had the opportunity to sit with a young girl who is a shadow of my younger self, and I had to talk to her about dreams, I would tell her to use her head and try to make the best choices, not just for the present but for the future as well.

- Iona

Dear Beautiful,

My name is Lola and I am in my 20s. I was born in Nigeria, but I now live in the United States.

I have a special gift of saying and seeing things before they occur. I've learned how much power words carry. It's indeed true that your thoughts lead to words that can either heal or hurt. I'm also very gifted in doing makeup and making others look beautiful.

I'm passionate about God. If I had not known him, there really would not have been anything else to be passionate about. After finding him, I realized I love caring for people. I'm also passionate about interior design, especially making a home look beautiful.

If I not could love the way I should, my life would be meaningless; I would feel hopeless and lost. I would do everything else but find no joy in it. Some people choose career, relationships and money over God, but after realizing that choosing God will mean having every other thing come easy, I decided to pursue Him. It has been the best decision I've had to make in my life. Nothing beats it, absolutely nothing.

As a child, I feared men the most because I was sexually abused as a child. It traumatized me so much. As a teenager, I feared the idea of dating, and the fear persisted when someone I dated betrayed my trust and threatened my safety. As a young woman, I fear getting hurt if I ever get the nerve to let love in because of my past experiences.

After being sexually abused and enduring physical abuse when I decided to give love a chance, I lost myself completely because the damage caused to my heart had been so much. I didn't want to date again, and I certainly had a different view of men in general. However, my past does not—and will not—define who I am.

My past is still a part of me, and the only thing I will allow it to do is to push me to be the very best I can be. My past will not be an excuse for failure. If I fail in any aspect of my life, it would be so I can learn and move forward to becoming great.

The greatest gift I was given by a friend was a Bible. When it was hard to heal from post-traumatic stress disorder, when I had lost myself completely and had no one else to run to, I believed that if there is indeed a God, I would get to know him and I wouldn't give up on the quest to find him. Well I did find him, and I have been healing gradually from all the hurt and pain I had gone through. I am finding myself; I have found my purpose. Where purpose is not known, abuse is inevitable. I no longer have any fear except for the fear of losing touch with God.

"Seek first the kingdom of God and his righteousness, and everything else will be added unto you." This is my favorite verse in the Bible and it has worked greatly for me. It was hard being vulnerable, it was hard letting go of all my wants and needs, but there is nothing like finding joy in God. It's a feeling I can't describe; you will have to experience it yourself.

If I could speak to my younger self, I would tell her she is beautiful, intelligent, capable of doing anything she sets her mind to, a fighter, a hero, loved, and the mother of all nations.

One of my biggest challenges was submitting to authority. Because I lived in an environment that considers abuse to be normal, I developed a defense mechanism that has made me not want to submit to leadership and authority, especially from the men in my life, such as my dad, uncle, or a male teacher. And if I did submit to authority, I would be so vulnerable that I would accept whatever was asked of me without objecting. It's either I'm not submissive or I'm too submissive to the point of being a victim of abuse. It was a battle in keeping the balance.

Before I knew God, I would usually call my friends to tell them about my struggles, but then they started to get tired of hearing the same stories. Some friends would make fun of or gossip about the things I shared with them, while others were going through hard times as well. I started feeling like I was a burden to them.

When I couldn't talk to anyone else, I turned to God. I tell him about my struggles first, and I think twice about sharing them with my parents or friends later. A problem shared is half-solved. That's why if I have a need, I don't hesitate to tell my trustworthy friends, but only after I pray about it first. Handing over your struggles to God is the best and wisest decision you can make in trying times. Trust me, it works like magic every single time.

I feel I hold myself back with my self-defeating thoughts. I sometimes feel like I'm not good enough or there is just something wrong with me. I am sometimes very hard on myself. I also hold myself back by not being flexible, reading too much into things, and worrying about little things.

I have tried to push myself forward by learning that God did not make a mistake in creating me, and I had to accept the hard truth that it's okay to be absolutely different from everyone else. It's okay to be who I am. It's okay to be weird, bubbly, loud, beautiful, and crazy about God. I realize it will be hard to convince people of who I am if I don't believe I can be comfortable in being who I am.

I see myself as a beautiful and a wonderful creation, and I see myself growing physically, emotionally and spiritually. I see myself as a woman that has become successful because she has chosen to not let her past determine her present and her future, and I thank God for the woman he is shaping me into. I feel like others see me as crazy, unpredictable, slow, mysterious, playful, intelligent, courageous, brave, funny, nice, sweet, beautiful, always moody, confident, outspoken, and someone who never smiles.

Self-acceptance is a big issue for me, and I'm still working on it. Being in any abusive relationship means you must have been manipulated and controlled. If you were a confident and outspoken person before going into that relationship, you will find it hard to go back to who you used to be after you've come out of it.

I am most comfortable when I am acting like myself, and I have learned to focus on my strengths and work on my weaknesses, while also enjoying the process. I look in the mirror each day and say positive words to myself. I realize that I am the only one who can make myself happy, and I am the only one that can make myself sad. I am the only one that can make myself feel like a failure and I am the only one that can make myself feel like a champion.

I may not be perfect or a genius, but I am willing to accept change, and I am willing to accept the challenge of becoming who I truly am. I have stopped comparing myself to other people because I realize God purposely created each person in a unique and different way, and no matter how much you want to imitate someone else's life, you can never have it all. I am in the process of loving myself fully without being selfish or conceited—loving myself because God loves me.

What I value most in life is my relationship with God. His presence is like heaven to me. It's something I fear losing because it could be so easy to lose with the distractions of this world. Living in the world but not being a part of it is a great challenge, but quite rewarding.

There is absolutely nothing like his presence—it makes life so much easier.

Beautiful, I think self-image, self-acceptance and good parental guidance are all struggles for you. The media has portrayed women in unedifying ways.

If I had an opportunity to sit with a young girl, I would tell her, "Never ever limit herself. If you never try, you will never succeed. If you have no one to push you, push yourself, because at the end of the day, it will be you to reap what you've sown. Set your priorities straight. It's either you want to read your books now and enjoy living comfortably, or you want to listen to your iPod all day, miss homework and school, and spend time with friends, only to end up years later hustling until you die (harsh but true). Why not hustle to do the necessary things while you have all the opportunities to do so now? The older one gets, the harder the hustling becomes."

It's only by God's grace that people who have missed those opportunities get them back. Nothing should ever stop you from achieving your goals. If you set your mind to achieve it, you will. You are what you say to yourself. If you say you are a failure, then you become a failure; if you say to yourself you are intelligent, then you will become intelligent. Dreams don't come true unless they are worked on. It comes with a lot of sacrifices and discipline, and sometimes you might have to be the one to discipline yourself.

- *Lola*

Dear Beautiful,

My name is Monir and I am in my 40s. I was born in Iran and I live in the United States.

When I was growing up, I wanted to be a star and a model. Today, I am a clinical social worker. I am empathetic and I have a real sharp intuition if I tune in and keep my spirit fed with prayers and meditation.

My passions vary. I am passionate about my spiritual quest as a member of the Baha'i Faith, where service to humanity is our duty, including bringing neighborhood activities to communities where children, youth and parents can be empowered with spiritual tools to take charge of their own lives, communities and spiritual growth.

I am also passionate about empowering and encouraging others, including my daughter, my staff and my clients. I am passionate about music, dancing, and going to the beach, although I have not done much of these lately due to a very intense work schedule. When doing the things I am passionate about, I feel alive, invincible and powerful, but humble. I can't follow most of my passions regularly, and mostly I feel tired, lethargic and at times depressed when I am unable to do so.

As a young woman, what I feared most was a broken heart and a man's anger, because my dad had a temper. I also feared being abandoned. Today, I sometimes feel less vulnerable to my fears. I think that's why I ended up being so independent—I alone can take care of myself and raise my child. But maybe the reason why I don't have a partner in my life to take care of me is because I learned early on not to rely on anyone. Or possibly because of being let down, I just try to do it all myself.

If I spoke to my younger self, I would tell her, "You are okay just the way you are and you are good enough." As a woman, one of my biggest challenges has been meeting a compatible man. In order to combat this, I've decided to not settle, have faith, try to take better care of myself, and stay positive (although I'm not very successful at doing all of those all the time). But I also try to surrender to the will of God.

When things get difficult, I seek help from my sister and my friends (there aren't that many people but I am grateful for the ones I do have). I hold myself back by not valuing myself enough, not taking better care of myself, not eating right, not exercising enough, not meditating enough, not doing enough yoga, and not relaxing enough.

I push myself forward by praying, being selective of my surroundings in order to avoid negativity, and reading motivating and positive literature. I see myself as hardworking, driven, tired, compassionate, and at times too emotional. In terms of how others see me, I'm not sure—perhaps crazy, confident, sweet, outspoken, mean, and bossy.

The way I work on self-acceptance is by putting my hand on my heart and repeating this prayer, "In him let the trusting trust." I also tell myself, "You are okay just the way you are," although most times, I have difficulty accepting that.

What I value most in my life is my role as a mother, my religion, my family, my friends, and my health. It might sound cliché, but as I get older, these values become more important in a deeper sense. All these values center on love. So I guess, I mostly value love.

Beautiful, I believe your biggest struggles are self-image and self-value. What I believe contributes to those struggles are the media, fashion, music, and lack of spiritual (not necessarily religious) identity.

If I had the opportunity to sit with a young girl who is a shadow of my younger self, I would tell her, "Your dreams can come true as long as you believe in yourself and accept the good in you. Dreams can change as we evolve but as long as you stay centered, you will be okay."

- *Monir*

Dear Beautiful,

My name is Carlie and I am in my 60s. I was born in St. Vincent and now I live in the United States.

When I was growing up, I wanted to be a nurse. Today, I am a nurse. My special gift is the ability to keep things simple. I am passionate about work and family. Life consists of joys, disappointments, frustrations, and moving on. If I could not do the things I am passionate about, I think I would adjust somehow.

Although I have a difficult time remembering much of my childhood, the fears that I did have were of failure and loneliness. But now, I don't worry so much anymore about those things. If I did have the opportunity to go back and speak to my younger self, I would say to her, "I love you, you are good, and you are important; life will be okay."

In order to combat life's challenges, I try to stay optimistic and keep hope alive. I believe that somehow, tomorrow will be better. When things get difficult, I turn to family, friends, quiet, solitude and peace within, and gratitude for the good things that I have. I hold myself back through my self-doubt. So in order to push myself forward, I work on being optimistic and remembering the good things, especially the successes.

I see myself as someone who feels good about herself. I have learned to forgive my mistakes. My life is worthwhile. I feel that sometimes others may see me as being too simple. Self-acceptance is something I work on every day through prayer, forgiveness, and seeing others' weaknesses by accepting them. I have learned to value myself most in life; I believe that it is the only way to keep life in perspective.

Beautiful, I believe your biggest struggles probably include too much exposure, too much freedom, and too much influence from the world. I believe that lack of family structure and lack of direction contribute to those struggles.

If I had the opportunity to sit with a young girl who is a shadow of my younger self, my words would echo the essence of what I said earlier, "Trust and believe in God or prayer. Believe that you are good and worthwhile. Love yourself. Use the quiet spaces and solitude to recuperate spiritually. Believe that life will be better tomorrow. Believe that you are loved, but most importantly, love yourself."

- Carlie

Dear Beautiful,

My name is Solange and I am in my 30s. I was born in the United States where I currently reside.

When I was growing up, I wanted to be pediatrician, a singer, a magician, or president of the United States. As a child, my parents always told me that I could do anything that I wanted to do when I grew up, and I believed them. Today, I am a pediatrician.

I am a very sensitive person. There were points in my life where I saw this as a liability, and I've often been told that I need to have a thicker skin. However, now I realize that I am acutely able to see a situation from other people's point of view. As a result of this sensitivity, I am very compassionate. It helps when working in a team, negotiating deals with employers, and engaging with family. Also, when I am passionate about something, my passion can be contagious and I often easily engage and excite others.

What I am passionate about now is serving those that are underserved in some way. Often, within the field of medicine, minorities and children are not focused on. For example, drug development has not focused on children, which presents challenges for children in obtaining safe and effective medications for their illnesses. Additionally, minorities have poorer health outcomes than their white counterparts in many of the major causes of mortality in the United States. I am interested in working to ensure that studies and programs are addressing and focusing on these groups.

When doing the things I'm passionate about, I feel inspired and ready to take on challenges, and work to change the most vexing issues that I see in society. If I could not do those things I would feel disenchanted and disoriented, and I would ask myself whether this is God's purpose for my life.

As a young child, I was fearless and figured that most of what I wanted would come to pass. As a teenager, I was at times concerned about whether I would get into a certain college and get a scholarship to attend my college of choice. As a young woman, while I was working hard to become a physician, I found it more difficult to strike a balance between my personal and professional lives—I wondered whether I would find love.

In my current life, my concern about striking balance in my life persists, but I continue to manage it. Although I would love to find a life partner and build a family with him, I recognize that God has me on the path that I am on for a reason, and ultimately I continue to work on trusting God's direction in my life.

If I could go back and speak to my younger self, I would quote her some words from Vivian Greene: "Life isn't about waiting for the storm to pass. It's about learning to dance in the rain."

Beautiful, follow your passion of pursuing medicine and public health (if this is your passion), but stop and smell the roses. Date, figure out what you like and love in a man, and experience life. It is okay to fall down a few times because all of life involves a series of falls, whether you are successful or not. The test is how you rise from those falls.

One of my biggest challenges has been overcoming my shyness, especially when dating or interacting with the opposite sex in a social setting. Another challenge for me, which I have been improving on, is saying what I really want. In order to combat those challenges, I have put myself into social settings periodically to meet others.

I still am shy and often feel awkward, but it gets easier with practice. I surround myself with others who are able to say what they want kindly and delicately, but clearly, and emulate them when applicable. When things get difficult for me, I seek out help from other friends who are more comfortable and adept in these situations.

I do feel like I sometimes hold myself back through self-doubt and procrastination. Some of the things I do to push myself forward include meditation and surrounding myself with positive and supportive people.

When I look at myself, I see a kind and fair woman who enjoys intellectual stimulation. I believe others may see me as uptight at times, and fun-loving at times. At my best, I am beautiful and elegant. In order to work on self-acceptance, I do daily meditations and affirmations. In life, the thing that I value most is my time.

Beautiful, I believe your biggest struggles include self-image, believing in yourself, and knowing that your dreams matter. What contributes to those struggles are the images in the media because many of them are not realistically achievable by the average woman.

If I could have the opportunity to sit with a young girl who is a shadow of my younger self, my words to her would be, "Go for it with all of your heart, my dear. You will fall down at times, but get up again. You may feel as though you are straying away from the path, but remember that God uses *everything* for good for those who love him and have been called according to his purpose."

- Solange

Dear Beautiful,

My name is Jenise and I am in my 40s. I was born in Washington, D.C., USA.

When I was growing up, I did not know what I wanted to be, but I knew that I wanted to help people. Today, I am a clinical social worker, and I feel that everyone has special gifts.

It should be a never-ending journey to the discovery of your true gift. People say that I am special because I care greatly for everyone's happiness. I am grateful to have had 43 years of life to work on my special gifts to the world. I am very passionate about helping young people find their true selves. When I was a teenager, I needed help with finding my positive energy, and now I have the pleasure to motivate and encourage young people with their paths to a successful life. My parents thought that there was something wrong with me and I was not 'acting right'. So they made me see a clinical social worker to find out how to 'fix me'. I went reluctantly, but I felt even worse to think that something must have been wrong with me.

Over time, I understood my feelings and learned some new techniques to deal with my issues. I am thankful to my parents for wanting to make things better for me, instead of ignoring me or sweeping my problems under the rug.

It brings light to my heart to know that one encouraging word, a smile, or a hug can help a young person move past a challenging situation. I have worked long hours in stressful jobs for financial stability, with very few rewards. It made me feel like I was not doing what God wanted me to do. It felt like a betrayal of my God-given talents.

Being misunderstood is what I fear the most. I want people to see me for who I am now, and who I am growing to become. I still feel like people do not understand me, but now I just have to be clearer, louder, and more specific. If I was able to go back and speak to myself, I would make sure that I lived more, loved more, experienced everything, and stopped to see the sun rise and set every day.

One of my biggest challenges has been being able to put myself first. To honor yourself is a way to celebrate the person that you are becoming. When I have challenges, I listen to music and write poetry. I always wrote in my journal but I never let anyone see it. But I have since realized that in order to be heard, you must speak. So now I help young girls speak through poetry and spoken word.

I used to allow challenges to consume me, but being stressed out about my problems did not make the problems go away. Now, I take one day at a time, write a plan, and pray. I always prayed when things got difficult, but you have to pray and have faith in your prayer.

Self-doubt and failure hold me back from accomplishing more of what I want in life. Being still and meditating helps me become more focused and to push forward in accomplishing my dreams. It is extremely hard to be still, but it helps me to listen to my positive inner voice.

I see myself as God's child. I am flawed, funny, fabulous, and full of love and light. Sometimes I feel like people don't see me and they treat me like I am invisible. It's a hard pill to swallow, but I just keep on moving forward with my head held high. Self-acceptance is a journey that takes a lifetime. Little by little, if you listen closely to your inner self, you can accept what you are hearing.

I value my family the most in my life. I felt very empty and lost as a young girl. Not because I did not have a loving family, but because I felt like I did not belong. I was adopted as a baby, and I was blessed to have the most supportive parents. But being adopted is an unknown situation that you can't fix. I was empty on the inside, but tried to hide it with a smile on the outside. I still struggle with that today. I have a ray of happiness around me, to light up someone else's day, but I feel empty on the inside.

Beautiful, I feel like your struggles today are no different from when I was growing up. You want someone to listen to you, hold you, accept you, walk in your shoes, and not judge you. We have made the struggle more complicated by repeating the same mistakes with each generation. Young people are supposed to be motivated to learn and encouraged to strive to accomplish more than their parents. I feel that we are losing the strength that is within our young girls by being passive-aggressive towards our responsibilities as parents, guardians, and role models.

If I had a chance to sit with a young girl who is a shadow of my younger self, I would sit and listen. I would open my heart to hear her spirit, and help her find whatever she is looking for. Dreams are conceived in your sleep; take the time to reach down deep into your soul, find your true self, and then act upon it. I am alive and at peace in my life today because I never stopped listening to my true self.

- Jenise

FLIGHT 4: THE CREATORS

I believe that the ability to create artistically is one of the best gifts a human being can possess. As a child, I appreciated music and poetry, and I loved to draw and paint. As I've grown into a woman, I have appreciated creativity and artistry even more. If my spirit is ever broken, music heals, as it has so many times in my life. I have friends who are so creative and artistic that it oozes out of their pores. My letter is one of the letters in this chapter, but I really do enjoy reading and re-reading the ones from the creative minds that make up my circle and make up my world. That makes my heart happy.

"To create art with all the passion in one's soul is to live art with all the beauty in one's heart."
- Aberjhani

Dear Beautiful,

My name is Shona and I am in my 40s. I was born in St. Vincent and the Grenadines, but I now live in the United States.

When I was growing up, I first wanted to be a flight attendant, and then as I got older I wanted to be a writer, a singer, or an artist of some kind. Once I got to college, I was encouraged to be more 'practical' so I thought of becoming a lawyer. After applying to law school and not getting in, I decided to change course and enter the business world. Today, I am a communications/publications professional, an artist, and an entrepreneur.

I've always considered myself someone with whom God was generous when it came to special gifts. In the artistic realm, I have the gift of being able to see beauty in photography. As a writer, I am able to bring separate thoughts together. As a communicator and public speaker, I have been able to share messages and tell stories that bring to life the thing we all desire to do—to be our better selves.

I am passionate about telling the stories of our generation and about being a voice for young people. I am also passionate about my family, friends and loved ones, and the things that bring me great joy. Most importantly, I am passionate about finding balance in my life, finding a space where I can create, where I can give the best of me, where I can fail and know that it's okay as long as the lesson is learned, and where I can succeed and quietly rejoice in it.

Life would not be the same for me if I wasn't able to do the things I feel passionate about, and I have indeed experienced that before. There have been times when I lost the zest to do the things I love because I was dealing with mild bouts of sadness or depression; I would feel that there was a hole that needed to be filled. I am haunted by my dreams when I don't go after that which I should. I

was that teenager and young adult who would be awakened out of her dreams so that she could write them down, and later, bring an idea or a memory to life in a poem.

If I could no longer do the things I am passionate about, I would be lost—plain and simple. Earlier in my life, I tried to hide a little bit about who I was. This book is, in some way, my 'coming out'. I am no longer afraid to be who I am, and that's someone who is full of dreams—some that are too bold to be verbalized—but I know that in the deepest part of my subconscious, when I am alone, there is a series of words and mantras that spontaneously leave my brain and attach to my lips. I know that I have to follow my passion, regardless of how others may view me.

Other than ghosts and possibly the idea of death, as a young person, I always feared that I would not be able to attain the dreams I desired most because I was financially poor. My family has always been spiritually rich, but money was always a problem for us. I also feared that I would not be able to articulate what it was that I wanted to do and get the support needed to do it. I also feared being put into a box that didn't reflect me. This last fear is something I have realized in my current life and something that I try very hard to fight. I know now that my spirit or my desires cannot be put into a box; my dream span is much too big for that.

I feel that those fears are slowly burning away. Although I still get choked up speaking up for myself, I do so more often than not. I know now that I need not fear the things I cannot control, for it is that idea of controlling things that gets us all into trouble. Letting things happen on their own is usually the best approach.

If I could go back and speak to my younger self, I would tell her to not be so afraid and to take a few more chances. I would also tell her to not sweat the small stuff so much, because after all, in the perspective of the world and the universe, it is just small stuff.

I believe that one of my biggest challenges is being able to challenge things and situations without being considered rebellious. What I find interesting is that if I were a man saying the things I do and challenging the things that do not make sense, I would be praised. I believe that gender inequality is something that I will always experience but something I will always challenge.

In order to combat the challenges that come before me, I try to find creative outlets. I try doing things that relax my mind and keep me calm. Photography and writing have been a great way to divert my attention, even though I may not share my writings with anyone. I also seek guidance from the people in my life whom I consider to be mentors.

When things get difficult I tend to retreat a bit; I get very quiet and I can sometimes internalize things. I may share those difficulties with someone if I think it's the right time. However, when I do decide to combat them, I have a very small circle of friends whom I talk to, along with a couple members of my immediate family who I confide in. It's important for me to find people in whom I can confide.

I feel like I hold myself back in that I always seek to have a perfect outcome in whatever I do. I think the artist in me does not always allow me to be satisfied. There is usually a vision I have for something, whether it's a piece of poetry, taking a photograph or designing something. There is always a path and there is always an end result, and sometimes it's not what I hoped, so I may go back to it again and again. There have always been times when I tell myself I am not good enough and wonder what if people laugh or don't see my vision the same way. I have struggled with this for some time, but I am learning to understand that not everything I do will be liked the same way by everyone. It's a daily challenge. I try to be happy in my imperfection and find a spiritual balance.

I see myself as someone who is constantly growing, who is constantly searching, and who is constantly thinking about ways in which things can be better.

I see myself as someone searching to find ways to just be in the present moment and enjoy it for what it is. I see myself as someone who is trying to accomplish things, not just for my own satisfaction, but in order to help others along the path. For the most part, I feel like others see me as accomplished. I feel like they see me as a driven and passionate person.

In order for me to work on self-acceptance, I meditate and I talk to myself about not wanting to be compared to anyone else. My grandmother used to always say that you should never be envious of anyone for what they have because you don't know how they achieved it. In many ways, I think I try not to compete with anyone because I don't know what their journey was. I can only try to take steps in my own life journey. Although I have been gifted with many talents, there are still some things I know I will never be able to do well, like math!

What I value most in life is life itself. I value knowing that my family and friends are living good lives, free of stress and strife. I value individual moments with the people I love. I am an extrovert at times, but there is the side of me that is very introverted and would rather spend one-on-one time with people because I want to get to know them, without distractions.

I believe that girls and boys today have many fears and many struggles, but for you, Beautiful, they seem to be magnified. Some of your fears may include: not fitting in; not being beautiful enough; not being smart enough; not having enough money; not having fathers; being different; loving too much; not being loved enough; not having the right support; not giving yourself time; giving too much of yourself; not having lived enough; or being lost in your creativity, or lack of it.

I believe that the way we are brought up contributes to those fears. If you have a solid home life—one where you are allowed to be yourself and be creative and think independently—I think a lot can be achieved. I think there is a strong need for us to be accepted by the outside world, but the outside world can be harsh. I think that being satisfied with who you are, knowing that you can do a lot even though there may be limitations, is a healthy way to be.

If I could sit and talk with a young girl who is a shadow of my younger self, I would tell her to believe more in herself. I would tell her to let go of the hurt inside and to walk in her own beliefs. I would tell her that a missing parent does not make her weak or unloved. I would tell her that not being the brightest in class does not mean she is not worthy. I would tell her that learning to love and nourish her creative side is a gift, a gift that many are not blessed with. I will tell her that being a dreamer is okay, that there comes a time however when you have to stop following your dreams and start leading them.

- *Shona*

Dear Beautiful,

My name is Changamiré and I am in my 40s. I was born in the United States where I currently reside.

When I was growing up, I wanted to be a pilot and a mechanical engineer. Today, I am a recording artist, concierge, and marketing assistant.

My voice—both literally and figuratively—is my special gift. The timbre of a voice is unique to each individual, but people seem to love my voice's timbre. And figuratively speaking, my voice—that is, what I have to say—places love and fairness at the forefront. Other special gifts, which may be my favorite, are the ability to communicate with people from any walk of life, and the capacity to bring people from all walks of life together.

I am now passionate about living a happy life. This primarily means being more present at home and with family and friends than at work. Also, I have made changes so that my work makes me happy. It now involves touching lives in personal and meaningful ways versus material ways. When doing the things I am passionate about, I am happy, happy, happy!

I just recently made the change from living a life for income to living a more meaningful life. I thought the income provided the meaningful life. And it did for a while. But then the work to acquire the income became too rigorous, and the environment too volatile. At the other end of the spectrum were the things that I loved— music, family and friend gatherings, and philanthropy—that I could only do occasionally when I was not exhausted. I felt miserable.

Looking back into my childhood, I was a sick child, always in hospitals. I feared physical pain during that age. As a teenager and a young woman, I feared not fitting in. Peer pressure greatly affected me. Even today, although I am in great health, I still hate physical pain! But I no longer care about keeping up with the Joneses. I love my style, my heart, and the opportunity to have exchanges with family, friends and associates, regarding those things.

If I could go back and speak to my younger self, I would tell myself to remember those times when I was told—by square parent types— that I was amazing, but to disregard who the words came from. I would ask that I at least consider the possibility that those words were true and carried weight. Conversely, I would tell myself to remember those times when I was told in a variety of ways—by cool kid types—that I did not fit in, and to examine more closely who the words came from.

One of my biggest challenges has been achieving work-life balance and life-me balance. Leaving the nine-to-five lifestyle has resolved most of these challenges. I know I must have me time—whether through exercise, hanging out with friends, or being a couch potato—in order to maintain a happy and healthy lifestyle, so that I can be there for those around me.

When things get difficult, I seek out help from my husband and close friends. If I am in a situation when I cannot get to them but need help right away, I go someplace where I can be alone—perhaps on a bench in front of the building where I work, in my car, a park, a bathroom stall, wherever—and reflect on the situation with my higher power in mind. This means that the decision or resulting action will lie within doing the right thing.

I hold myself back in that I think small. My mentality is that! One takes small steps. I am also very loyal, and this has held me back on occasion. In order to push myself forward, I secretly do big things. I call or send letters to celebrities or try to get meetings with big music or event producers. With regard to a remedy for being too loyal, I am not looking for one.

I see myself as loving and creative. I feel like those close to me also see me as creative. Others see me as creative and a businesswoman.

I am working on self-acceptance, and I try to do the right thing. It comes down to whether I am being fair and loving, and this includes to myself. When I am fair and loving, I am okay with all of me. What I value most in my life is my family, friends and home.

Beautiful, I believe your biggest struggles are materialism, grand entitlement, and lack of manners. What I believe contributes to those struggles are popular culture, which promotes the former two, while all three should be taught, discussed and enforced at home.

If I had the opportunity to sit with a young girl who is a shadow of my younger self, I would say to her, "It is extraordinary that you want to be a pilot! And (years later), it is amazing that you are going to be a mechanical engineer! And if years from now you have found a new passion—some work that makes you extremely happy—let's explore that too!"

- Changamiré

Dear Beautiful,

My name is Marlene and I am in my 60s. I was born in the United States where I currently live.

When I was growing up I wanted to be a dancer. Today I am retired.

In terms of my special gifts, I like listening to people and asking them about their lives. I have become a better listener. I love to give handmade gifts to people who I love and care about. I find great comfort in helping people. I've become a better helper. I enjoy cooking for others. Seeing the expression on people's faces when they taste something they like is a gift to me. I know when I need time for myself, and I see that as a special gift. I value quiet time and the opportunity to enjoy being out in the world on my own, to be mindful and enjoy the present moment.

I am passionate about my family and friends, quilting, reading, trying new recipes, theater, travel, taking care of my home, learning about sailing, and trying to get beyond my fears. The feelings I get when I am doing the things I am passionate about vary. Sometimes I feel exhilarated, sometimes fearful, and sometimes exceptionally happy. If I could not do those things, I would be sad and maybe frustrated.

The thing I feared as a child was thinking I might do something wrong and get yelled at for it. As a teenager, I feared that I wasn't going to do as well as others in school. As a young woman, I feared that people who I thought were smarter than I was wouldn't like me.

The way I feel about those fears now is that they were probably common to children, teenagers and young women, so I was probably not so very different from other people in those age groups. The majority of people experience various fears until they learn they no longer have to.

If I could go back and talk to my younger self I would tell her, "You are absolutely fine and beautiful the way you are. I'm here for you whenever you feel afraid or insecure about anything. Let's check in with one another each day, okay?"

One of my biggest challenges is knowing that I was, and am, okay. In order to combat this challenge, I try to move beyond my fears by pushing outside of my boundaries or out of my comfort zone as a means toward personal growth.

When things get difficult, I turn to my health management organization that offers a weekly mindfulness group. Although it's not a place to speak about my challenges, I do find great comfort in mindfulness meditation and getting insight into ways to combat anxiety, fears and many other challenges. I also get help from talking with people I trust and who I know care about me. I have been able to find people in my life who listen well and with whom I feel comfortable sharing my feelings.

The way in which I hold myself back is that, out respect for other people's feelings, I almost always hold back my opinion when I think they are struggling with something which may be none of my business.

In order to push myself forward, I talk with someone I trust to offer help. I also meditate and do something I enjoy doing to clear my mind as a means toward getting myself in a better place. I also exercise.

I see myself as a work in progress, a person who wants to continue to be a student of life. I am helpful, and I am a person who has a good heart, likes to laugh, enjoys good music, likes to dance, enjoys art, enjoys a good book or gardening, likes good food, loves well, enjoys travel, and likes to be active. I believe the way people see me can be described as mostly the way I see myself.

I work on self-acceptance by being grateful for life. What I value most in life is my family and friends.

Beautiful, I think your biggest struggles include being confident in yourself and having the people in your life to help you achieve confidence.

If I had the opportunity to sit with a young girl who is a shadow of my younger self, I would say, "Try to think about what happiness is for you. It's up to you to be in charge of your happiness. Other people may offer suggestions or even push their ideas of what they think is good for you. But your happiness is your own job. Those other people who may be suggesting or pushing—your parents, siblings, friends, or your teachers—already have a job. Do something useful. Work hard and have fun doing the work. Surround yourself with good people."

- Marlene

Dear Beautiful,

My name is Sarah and I am in my 30s. I was born in and live in the United States.

When I was growing up, I wanted to be a singer. Today, I am a professional businesswoman who also does creative design.

As for my special gifts, I've been told that I am good at unifying people or bringing people together. I am still passionate about music. When doing the things I am passionate about, I feel happy, free, and connected with life. If I could not do those things, I would feel purposeless and empty.

The thing I feared the most when I was growing up was death. I used to have nightmares about my own funeral. Now that I'm older, I realize that life is about what you do with it, and the joy you've been able to bring to others. Today, I thank God for a new day and ask him for his guidance every day. I have been through some things in my life that confirm that I am a child of God, and so this makes me no longer fear death; I know it is all part of a greater purpose and timing that I have no control over. I can only take comfort in knowing that I am going to always strive to live my best life while I am here.

If I could go back and speak to my younger self, I would tell her, "Don't be afraid to listen to that soft voice within that is your spirit; it is your gift to the world from God. You have every right to listen to her and not be afraid, no matter what you do, as long as you can breathe in and breathe out. You will be okay and you will survive. To fight your fear is to fight for love. And that is the sole purpose why we are here."

I feel that one of my biggest challenges has been telling myself that I must get married and have children by a certain age. In

order to combat this challenge, I remind myself to trust the timing of my life.

When things get difficult for me, I pray, write in a journal, talk to friends, and spend time with family. I haven't been able to incorporate this into my schedule lately, but volunteer work is very therapeutic as well. Helping someone else should naturally make you feel good.

On a weekly basis, I set short goals for myself. As I check things off, I feel good and in control of my life and my future. This helps me to push myself forward. I see myself as a little funny and a little geeky.

With regard to self-acceptance, if I find myself having any negative thoughts on my self-image, I try to stop them early and meditate. What I value most in life is laughter.

Beautiful, I feel that your biggest struggle is self-image; this is especially so for young black girls. I believe the media contributes to that struggle.

If I had the opportunity to sit with a young girl who is a shadow of my younger self, I would say to her, "Dreams are like looking through a crystal ball of your spirit. It's okay to follow them and it's also okay if they change as you grow and become a different person."

- Sarah

FLIGHT 5: THE COMMUNICATORS

Having the ability to communicate well is one of the greatest gifts a person can have. In today's society, I believe we are all becoming more frequent communicators through the explosion of social media.

When I was a young girl, I hardly ever heard of women who were in the communications field. The works we studied were mostly by or about men. It was not until I got to college that my eyes were opened to the strong, intelligent women who occupied so many areas of communications, including writing, editing, journalism, and web content management.

Verbal communication is so essential today, and as a public speaker and poet, I know how much emotion and the ability to bring awareness to issues can cultivate a new and deeper level of understanding between all of us. The written word—the understanding and crafting of it—is also important; it is needed in our society to help us also reach a greater level of understanding, and maybe quite possible, appreciation for each other.

As diverse as our world is and continues to become, it's important to have diversity amongst the communicators of our time, for it is diversity that drives innovation, and that is something we cannot live without.

"I'm a great believer that any tool that enhances communication has profound effects in terms of how people can learn from each other, and how they can achieve the kind of freedoms that they're interested in."
-Bill Gates

Dear Beautiful,

My name is Amanda and I am in my 30s. I was born and still live in the United States.

When I was growing up, I wanted to be a writer. Today, I am the marketing assistant for an arts center. I am also a member of my state's Disabilities Council, where I am thankful to have the opportunity to advocate for the equal rights and full inclusion of all people with disabilities.

God blessed me with a talent for writing. I was also blessed with the gift of encouraging others and a desire to share his love by serving people who are in need. I am passionate about helping others and making an impact in the world for Christ.

When doing things I am passionate about, I feel that God is using me to make a difference for his glory. However, when I can't do the things that I am passionate about, my physical disability has taught me many creative ways to overcome obstacles that I may encounter. My faith and wonderful family have also been an important part of successfully overcoming various obstacles.

When I was growing up, I was fearful that some of my peers might not accept me because of my disability. That is not a concern now.

If I could give advice to my younger self, I would tell her to stay true to herself and seek the advice of her family. Keep the faith and remember that with God, all things are possible! As a woman, I am constantly discovering that it is okay to be assertive and speak up for myself. My faith and my family help me to combat challenges that I encounter. When things become difficult, I always seek help from my wonderfully supportive and encouraging family, especially my mom and my most wonderful stepfather!

Fear and obstacles hold me back. To push myself forward, I seek God's wisdom. I also try new things and have new experiences, even when those experiences might be scary or difficult.

I see myself as someone who makes an impact for Christ by encouraging others and advocating for people with disabilities. I feel that others view me as a person who is loyal and helpful, as well as positive, encouraging and uplifting.

In my life, I value my relationship with Christ, my family and friends the most. I work on self-acceptance by maintaining a positive attitude, emphasizing my strengths, and discovering ways to overcome obstacles.

Beautiful, today you may struggle with developing a positive and realistic self-image. In my view, the media and the messages communicated in music and on television are the largest contributors in this struggle. If I could sit with a young girl, I would remind her to stay true to herself and her beliefs, to be positive, and to value the wisdom of her family and friends.

- *Amanda*

Dear Beautiful,

My name is Sandi D. and I am in my 40s. I was born and still live in the United States.

When I was growing up, I wanted to be either a veterinarian or a medical researcher. Today, I am an editor.

I have the gift of being detail-oriented yet able to grasp the big picture. I love helping others, and I'm often asked to serve as team leader on the development of high-profile publications. I learn foreign languages easily and enjoy interacting with people from different cultures.

I love intercultural communications. I absolutely love learning about people from other cultures. Recently, I developed a passion for photography and painting. I was always made to feel like I was not the artistic one in the family, so I had no idea I could draw more than a stick figure.

When I am doing the things I am passionate about, I have a sense of fulfillment and supreme happiness. If I couldn't do those things, I would feel drained and tired. I feel restless when I meet people with whom I cannot share stories while learning more about them and the world.

When I was a young girl, I feared not having financial security. Although it was not in the forefront of my mind, it was something I was aware of, especially having grown up in a family of modest means. My mom didn't become financially comfortable until she reached her mid-forties.

As a child, I was aware that I didn't fit in with mainstream classmates. I was born in New York City and moved to Long Island when I was six. By first grade, cliques were already formed, and I was viewed as an outsider. I sought out those who were different like I was. My best childhood friends included a French-American whom I met when I was nine, and a high-school friend who is American but grew up in Greece. These friends opened my world. My French-American friend's mother used to take us to see French movies at the local repertoire theater and at the local art museum. I can confidently say that not many girls in my class saw the movie, *Hiroshima, Mon Amour*!

I am more relaxed when I think of those childhood fears now. Money has never been particularly important to me, except as a means to do those things I love, such as travel. In terms of not fitting in, I am so happy that I never sought to conform to the norm, since I am happy remaining my true, authentic self.

If I could go back and speak to my younger self, I would say, "Don't stress out about not fitting in. Embrace the small group of friends you have and be happy. Also, don't be shy about trying out new endeavors. If you don't like it, the worst that can happen is that you decide it isn't your cup of tea, and you move on and find something more interesting. This applies to extracurricular activities, college majors, and later—if necessary—life partners. Do not settle for less!"

As far as challenges go, I am constantly expected to help others, which I enjoy. But in the workplace, this translates to being expected to manage people or projects without getting the proper title and financial recognition. I don't care so much about the title, but not being paid fairly is not good for one's self esteem, in my opinion.

To combat those specific challenges, I am currently working with a fabulous career coach. She is a positive force in my life. One of the books she recommended I read was the *Gifts of Imperfection* by Brené Brown. This book has helped me accept that I cannot be perfect and cannot always help everyone, and that I have to set boundaries.

When things get difficult, my go-to person is my mom. She has always been there for me! She has a wide range of life experiences, from losing my seven-year-old brother in a drowning accident to raising two young girls as a single parent.

For the longest time, my fear of public speaking held me back. As I have gotten older, I am less shy and reserved. The fear stems from worrying about not being perfect and making a fool of myself in front of a group of people. But when you realize people are there because you have knowledge to impart, it can be liberating.

My love of people is really what has helped me to push myself forward. I love to collaborate on teams, so being able to speak confidently about my area of expertise has helped assuage my fear of public speaking. I recently took an in-depth career and personality assessment, where the results clearly indicated that I am a blended energizer—that I am both an introvert and extrovert, but I need time alone to recharge my batteries. I have always seen myself primarily as an introvert, but realize that I really do love being with people—they just need to be interesting people.

I see myself as someone who is constantly on the go and who seeks continuous improvement. I am not perfect, and that is okay. I often think I could look better physically. Even when I have looked better physically, I was not aware of this. I realized this the other day when looking at my portrait made by an art teacher in Japan. I had no clue that I remotely looked like what he had portrayed. It was an eye-opener.

I think others are less harsh than I am in terms of how I think they see me. I suspect that at first I may come across as reserved, but as people get to know me, they realize that I would do anything for those who matter to me.

I am still working on self-acceptance, but I'm making great strides. I guess as one matures, a certain level of Zen sets in and one is able to lighten up and not be as self-critical. Also, as Oprah would say, I had an *Aha* moment when my health suffered during a particularly stressful time in my career. As a result, I have been working on finding ways to relax for the past few months, and I launched a blog, www.AllThingsRelax.com, to provide others with tips on how to relax. Self-acceptance comes easier when one is able to relax.

What I value most in life and cherish are my family and friends, and my two cats.

Beautiful, I think the whole self-image issue is still a challenge for you. You also struggle with the need to fit in. The media doesn't help with how women are portrayed. I think, though, that the tide is finally starting to change. I feel that moms with young boys are an important part of the equation as well. Moms can teach their sons that beauty is only skin deep and to value women who will inspire them to be better men.

If I had the opportunity to sit with a young girl who is a shadow of my younger self, I would tell her to never stop trying to reach for the brass ring. Never give up hope. Always strive to learn something new, to be kind to others, and do your best.

- Sandi D.

Dear Beautiful,

My name is Angela and I am in my 40s. I was born in and live in the United States.

When I was growing up, I wanted to be a fashion designer. Today, I am a web content manager, writer, video and print editor, and archivist.

I certainly feel like I have special gifts, including helping people feel joy, and making people feel comfortable with sharing personal stories. I am passionate about social justice, and when I am doing the things I am passionate about, I feel like I'm making a positive difference in the world. If I couldn't do those things, I would feel like I'm not fulfilling my true mission on Earth, which is service to others.

As a child, I feared being around other people. However I have learned to be more accepting of myself and have compassion for myself, which has helped me manage my social anxiety.

If I could go back and speak to my younger self, I would tell her, "The things that have happened in your family are not your fault. You deserve better. Also, things will improve for you as you grow older, I promise."

I feel that two of my biggest challenges have been learning to love and honor myself and exercising my right to express my authentic feelings. In order to combat those challenges, I pray and meditate. I also set high goals for myself and try to meet them. When things get difficult, I mainly turn to God, and he has always helped me.

The way in which I hold myself back is that I often I rely on the material world rather than the spiritual world for my security and peace. But in order to push myself forward, I visualize the kind of life I want and am capable of having. I am also constantly learning new things in all areas of my life.

I see myself as someone who has worked hard to overcome some personal challenges and who has high hopes for her future. I feel as though people see me as a person who is honest, friendly, loyal to her friends, and committed to addressing societal inequalities in any way she can.

I work on self-acceptance by acknowledging the unconditional love, grace and inner joy that comes from the God within. What I value most in life are my family, friends and relationships in general.

Beautiful, I think that your biggest struggles are low self-esteem, hyper-sexuality (promoted by the society), and a general lack of adult guidance. Sexism, racism, educational and economic inequality, greed, and excessive materialism are what contribute to those struggles.

If I had the opportunity to sit with a young girl who is a shadow of my younger self, I would tell her that she should spend time daydreaming, and write down her dreams and draw and develop poster boards of her dreams. Once that vision is imprinted in the soul, it can be turned into reality, but you have to believe it can happen first.

- Angela

Dear Beautiful,

My name is Micheline and I am in my 40s. I was born in the U.S. Virgin Islands and I reside in the United States.

When I was growing up, I wanted to be a lawyer, a journalist, and an author. Today, I am a web content specialist.

My special gifts to the world include being good with words—I'm a good editor and writer—being a good listener, and being hospitable and welcoming.

What I'm passionate about is something that I'm struggling with now. I love creative writing, and I've always wanted to write fiction. However, I've found that as I've gotten older and attained the responsibilities of adulthood, I've put that goal on the back burner for several years. It's still something that I'd like to get back to doing on a regular basis.

Other than that, I'm passionate about spending quality time with family and friends. When I'm doing these things, I feel fulfilled, productive and happy. If, for whatever the reason, I could not do these things, I would feel frustrated, stuck and unhappy.

As a young woman, the thing I most feared was not fitting in, not being popular, or not being liked. But now I understand that the most important thing is to know God loves you, to love yourself and not worry so much about what other people think of you.

If I could go back in time and speak to my younger self, I would tell her, "It's okay to be yourself, even if you're different from your peers. God made us all unique, and you have to embrace the person he's made you, with all your strengths and weaknesses."

Two of my biggest challenges have been overcoming low self-esteem and overcoming my fear of change and failure. I've come a long way, but those are things I still have to work on from time to time.

In order to combat those challenges, I pray, seek advice from trusted family members and friends, and challenge myself to do things even when I'm scared or uncertain. And when things get difficult I seek help from God, my church family, my parents, siblings, and friends.

Like many, I do feel like I hold myself back. Sometimes I let fear keep me from trying new things. In order to push myself forward, I challenge myself to try new things despite being afraid or uncertain. I read inspirational books and articles. Most times, once I've done something despite being scared, I find that my fears were unfounded.

I see myself as a loving, nurturing person who wants to fulfill God's purpose for her life. I am by no means perfect, but I'm a work in progress. I definitely see the progress I've made, although I recognize

I still have a ways to go. I hope that others also see me as loving and nurturing. I'd like them to see me as a confident, self-assured woman.

I think self-acceptance comes easier with age and experience. However, I find that it helps to read and memorize scriptures about how much God loves me and how he sees me. Also, while it's important to work on your weaknesses, it's important to also acknowledge and not diminish your strengths. What I value most is God's blessings in my life and the love and support of my family and friends.

Beautiful, today you face a lot of challenges to your self-esteem due to unrealistic body images and monolithic standards of beauty portrayed in the media. Many times, you also have to contend with the idea that women are not suited for or welcome in certain careers, such as science, technology, engineering and math. Unfortunately, sometimes family members, friends, teachers, and the media contribute to those struggles.

If I had the opportunity to sit with a young girl who is a shadow of my younger self, I would encourage her to pursue her dreams vigorously and not to give up on them, even when there are obstacles or delays. Also, I'd tell her that sometimes new dreams emerge, and to not be afraid to change direction or refocus if she feels led to do so. Finally, I'd tell her not to let the fear of failure keep her from pursuing her dreams.

- Micheline

FLIGHT 6: THE ORGANIZERS

I sometimes look at life as a series of unrelated events that come together to form unity. For the women who are mothers, there is a lot of coordination that happens in caring for children and taking care of a home and family. For women who choose careers where there has to be coordination of efforts, there is a level of give-and-take and working in collaboration with others, which can sometimes be a difficult undertaking.

Some of us are born with the gift of being able to turn chaos into calm; others are not so lucky and need help excelling in that area. The best coordinators I know are the ones that ask questions of others, and they are curious to know how others think and how they can contribute. They are willing to hold their ideas and hear others' first. They are even sometimes willing to go with the ideas of others if they are better than the ones they envisioned. When it comes down to it, for them it's about the strength of the collaboration and the ability to cooperate and build a better reality.

"Cooperation over competition. If the world simply sees this statement, together we can begin our exploration of it. Simply seeing it is enough to create change."
-Réné Gaudette

Dear Beautiful,

My name is Samiha and I am in my 40s. I was born in Egypt and I now live in the United States.

When I was growing up, I wanted to be a teacher. Today, I am a program coordinator.

I am a very caring and giving person. I become energized by lending a helping hand and I've always been drawn to performing good work. It feels good, and I like to feel needed.

I am completely passionate about my daughters. From the moment they were born, I was transformed. I am best at being a mother. When I am doing things with them, I feel complete and satisfied. Not being able to spend time with them is something I couldn't even fathom; they are my life.

As a child, I feared losing my dad. He was ill with lung cancer and I lived in fear of him passing away. He eventually died when I was 13. As a teenager, I feared losing my boyfriend. I became very attached to him because he was my first love. I eventually lost him after dating for seven years. As a young woman, I always worried about losing my mom after my dad passed away. She passed away from a heart attack at age 52. It was a shock, really. I also always feared getting divorced. I had seen the early negative signs of a declining marriage, but I ignored them. I would lose my husband to divorce at age 40.

I've learned that loss is a part of life. It's a process we all have to go through. Loss is a terrible thing. You must grieve each loss and mourn until the stage of acceptance. With age comes maturity; with maturity comes acceptance; with acceptance comes wisdom.

If I could go back and speak to my younger self, I would tell her to stay in school. I dated at a young age and put my education on the back burner. I would tell my younger self to never compromise her education! It's the only thing that cannot be taken away from you. The other thing I would tell my younger self is, "Spend more time— lots of time—with your mom. When she passes away, you can't imagine how much you will miss her."

The biggest challenge I have faced is that as a minority, I have to work triple hard at everything. I have to prove myself at work. It's also a challenge being divorced. It's not easy raising two daughters alone, especially with the high standards that I have set for them.

In order to face some of those challenges, I pray, pray, and pray. The power of prayer is amazing. It's my shield, my protection, and my sanity. And when things get difficult, I seek help from God—our highest authority, our supreme being!

I hold myself back by sometimes thinking too much, analyzing too much, and weighing options too much. It would be good to just delve in without too much thinking.

In terms of pushing myself forward, it's always been good to acquire another degree or certification, or attend training courses. The more I learn, the more I can contribute in life. I always look for the next level to elevate myself.

I see myself as a good person. Sure, we can all improve our image, but I'm generally happy with myself. I'm not sure how others see me. I would hope they see the same thing, but I can't say for sure.

I think my religion plays a major role in my self-acceptance. My faith really keeps me grounded. What I value most in life are my children.

Beautiful, I would say that image-related struggles are the biggest for you: weight, hair and height. Then there are academic pressures arising from challenging courses, SAT scores, college-prep, internships, etc. Also, there are competing demands from smart phones and social media, and you have to balance everything else in life, such as school, sports, volunteer opportunities, part-time employment, and family time. Society, magazines and television ads are what contribute to your struggles—it's everywhere.

If I had the opportunity to sit with a young girl who is a shadow of my younger self, I would say to her, "You're beautiful, inside and out. Never settle. Do your best—your true best, and everything will fall in place. Never compromise your education. Learn, learn, and learn!

"Pray to God. Trust in Him; he's always with you. Treat others kindly; karma is very real! Don't hold grudges; forgive. It frees your soul. Your kids are top priority! Don't deviate from that path.

Marry someone who loves you more than you love them.

"Be extra good to your mother; heaven is found at her feet! Love your sibling; s/he is from the same stomach! Cherish good friendships; they are so important in life. Protect your credit; it's your reputation, and it's extremely important. Take good care of your health; always get annual checkups for early disease detection!"

- Samiha

Dear Beautiful,

My name is Sandra and I'm in my 60s. I was born in St. Vincent and the Grenadines, but today live in the United States.

When I was growing up, I wanted to be a flight attendant. Today, I am a church parish administrator.

I feel I have many special gifts that God has given me. As a young girl, I was able to take apart a piece of clothing and make it over. As I got a little older, I began to sew my own clothes without being taught how to do it. I can bake and decorate cakes without having been taught how to do that too. I do floral arrangements without having been taught, so I know that God has given me the ability to use my hands.

I am totally passionate about God and serving him in and around his House of Worship. When I am fulfilling this passion, I feel great joy. I feel happy and energetic. If I could not do those things, I would be sad; I cannot imagine not serving somehow.

What I feared most as a young person was the ocean, and it's a fear I still have today.

If I could go back and speak to my younger self, I would tell her, "You can do anything and everything, you are bright and beautiful, and God loves you."

One of my biggest challenges has been saying no. It is still difficult for me to say no, so it's something that still challenges me today.

When things get difficult and I need help, I go to God in prayer, and I also go to my family. What holds me back sometimes is that I doubt my abilities and myself. I don't know how to ask for help. In order to push myself forward, I pray and I tell myself I can do it. I ask God to give me the strength, and He does.

I see myself as an understanding, forgiving, compassionate and generous person. I believe some people see me as a pushover—that I can be easily fooled—while I feel others see me as a person who is easy to talk to and a loyal friend.

I have grown to accept who I am—a child of the King. I have realized that God made me the way that I am. I may not know everything or be able to do everything, but that's okay. What I value most in my life are my children, family and my friends.

Beautiful, I feel that your biggest struggle is self-acceptance. You are consumed with images you see on the television. I strongly believe that demographics and a lack of mentorship are what contribute to those struggles.

If I had the opportunity to sit with a young girl who is a shadow of my younger self, I would say to her, "Go for it; do not be afraid to do, say or be. You are a child of God, wonderfully made. God has given you what you need to be a success."

- *Sandra*

FLIGHT 7: THE WARRIORS

I strongly believe that all of the women featured in this book are warriors. They all have a story, they all have dreams, and they all want to fly high. But the woman in this chapter is versed in legal affairs and social issues.

As I mentioned in my own letter earlier on, I wanted to be a lawyer, but it was not in the cards for me. It's one of my dreams unfulfilled. I suppose there was just a part of me that wanted to help others in a legal capacity, but sometimes we don't get to choose our path; instead, our path chooses us.

"Until the great mass of the people shall be filled with the sense of responsibility for each other's welfare, social justice can never be attained."
-Helen Keller

Dear Beautiful,

My name is Karima and I am in my 40s. I was born in the United States where I currently reside.

When I was growing up, I wanted to be an attorney. Today, I am a corporate attorney and the founder and CEO of an executive consulting firm.

My special gifts include helping people to raise their standards, expectations and achieve results. I am very passionate about entrepreneurship, and when being entrepreneurial I feel invincible and blessed beyond measure.

If I could not work on the things I am passionate about, I would feel trapped, unhappy and unfulfilled.

As a young person, I was fearful of being unhappy and unsuccessful. But now those fears are no longer a part of my psyche or reality. In fact, if I could go back and speak to my younger self, I would say to her, "Sweetheart, I want you to know that God has blessed you with incredible gifts and a bright future full of unlimited opportunities too amazing to even comprehend. Believe in the universe of possibilities. Believe in yourself. Love yourself more—a lot more. Stretch your imagination, think outside the box, and don't be afraid to keep trying until you get what you want. Everything you want in this world is well within your grasp."

One of my biggest challenges has been an ever-evolving self-concept. In order to combat that challenge, I have learned to take it in stride. I am constantly learning, growing and making mistakes. I've learned that it's a natural part of being human, and as long as there is breath in my body, I can expect some form of evolution to take place. But with age and experience, I've learned to embrace it as a positive aspect of my conscious humanity.

When things get difficult for me, I seek help from my mom. She has incredible insight and doesn't judge.

There are times when I do hold myself back and I do that by second-guessing myself and procrastinating. Sometimes I get stuck in the muck and mire.

To push myself forward, I reframe and see myself as competent to do whatever I need to, and the second-guessing stops. With regard to my procrastination, I take baby steps towards goals, whatever they may be. Once I get the ball rolling, everything else seems to fall into place.

I see myself as a woman who is driven and prepared to do all that she can to live her best life. I feel like others see me as someone who is passionate, good-natured and sincerely loves people.

In order to work on self-acceptance, I do it day by day; it's a process.

What I value most in my life is freedom and happiness.

Beautiful, I feel that your biggest struggles are self-image and an overwhelming desire to fit in. What contributes to those struggles are social pressures to conform and the unfortunate stigmas associated with not meeting the rigors of whatever the categorical standard is.

If I had the opportunity to sit with a young girl who is a shadow of my younger self, I would say to her, "Dream big and never give up. Life is short, so don't spend it unhappy or contemplating whether you should take action. Take risks. Make mistakes. Do. Be. Love. Live life to the fullest and make the world a better place by your unique contributions.

- *Karima*

FLIGHT 8: THE BUILDERS

Women in technology are featured in this chapter. More and more, women are moving into the technology field, and I think that this is a wonderful thing and a change that young girls should embrace. I also studied technology; I have a second master's degree in information technology (IT) management. I have always been fascinated by how things work on the back end. My education was not focused on programming, but on managing the different parts of information technologies.

I think it's a beautiful thing when women are really involved in knowing how things work in the background. The women in this chapter are, in many ways, builders. They understand not just the technical side of things, but they see the bigger picture a lot clearer in life, and they are able to break things apart and put them back together in a most useful way, and that's the essence of who they are. They are, in some ways, bridging the understanding between man and machine.

**"One machine can do the work of 50 ordinary men.
No machine can do the work of one extraordinary man."**
-Albert Hubbard

Dear Beautiful,

My name is Lakshmi and I am in my 40s. I was born in India and live in the United States.

When I was growing up, I wanted to be a good, balanced human being who helped people in need. Today, I work in the IT field, and I am fortunate to be in a position to help others outside of work. I love to volunteer wherever possible. Currently, I cook and feed homeless people, and I teach foreign students.

My special gifts to the world are my kindness and generosity. I am passionate about performing acts of kindness and being a generous person, and when I am doing those things, I feel great. Nothing gives me more satisfaction than volunteering because I don't expect anything back. If I could not do those things, I would feel very empty.

As a child, I did not fear anything. As a teenager and young woman, I was too shy and I did not want to interact with anyone I didn't know. The way I feel about these fears now is that I thought I was foolish. I wish I were more open-minded during my teenage years.

If I could go back and speak to my younger self, I would tell her that there's no need to feel shy. Making new friends is a beautiful experience. There are several other people who go through similar experiences. By sharing your thoughts with others, it will help you realize that you're not alone.

One of my biggest challenges has been that I am too shy. Because I was too shy to make new friends as a teenager and young woman, it was challenging to make new friends. I overcame this challenge when I moved to the United States. I was new to the country, culture and language, and I didn't know anyone. So I didn't have any choice but to open up and make new friends.

When things get difficult in my life, I thank my husband who has helped me overcome shyness in meeting new people. I also thank my parents and siblings.

I feel like I've held myself back by trying to be perfect and fearing making a mistake. One of the things I do to push myself forward is to keep an open mind, knowing that I'm not alone.

I see myself as optimistic, content, and happy with myself at all times. I would think that others see me as confident and happy.

The way I work on self-acceptance is by being happy with who I am and with what I have. What I value most in life is my family and my other relationships.

Beautiful, I believe your biggest struggle is that you try to be someone else. I believe that the loss of self-confidence and personal growth contribute to those struggles.

If I had the opportunity to sit with a young girl who is a shadow of my younger self, I would say to her, "No need to fear. You're not alone. The sky is the limit. Keep an open mind and pursue your passions."

- Lakshmi

Dear Beautiful,

My name is Cheryl and I am in my 40s. I was born in the United States where I currently reside.

When I was growing up, I wanted to be an actress. Today, I am a systems integrator and implementer.

My special gift is that I am very analytical, which helps me to be a better software developer. It also helps when producing films.

At this stage in my life, I am passionate about a few things. They often change with each passing year, but for now, I'm passionate about finding someone special to settle down with, continuing to be successful at my career and expanding my business, and working with creative Christians on making films.

When I am doing the things I am passionate about, I feel exhilarated and free to be me, and I live life to the fullest. I feel like there's nothing I can't do or overcome. If I couldn't do the things I'm passionate about, it would be hard to find motivation and drive to get up and give 100 percent each day.

What I feared most when I was a young woman was being ridiculed by others based on my appearance—perhaps being too tall or too thin—and not being liked or accepted by others. To a degree, some of those fears have followed me into adulthood. Each day I have to stand up to them because I know I am bigger than my fears.

If I could go back and speak to my younger self, I would tell her to always follow her gut and first instinct. They are usually correct, even if they seem illogical or non-pragmatic.

Two of my biggest challenges have been professional speaking and vocalizing my accomplishments. It's so important that others see and hear about what you contribute and how much you are truly capable of. To combat those challenges, I take the time to vocalize more of what I've accomplished in meetings, on status reports, on my resume, and when networking with others.

When things get difficult, the person I seek out depends on what I'm having difficulty with. If it's a life decision, it would definitely be my mom. Her insight and prayers offer the support and confidence needed when at a crossroads.

I don't feel I hold myself back as much as I did in the past. I think I've always been a humble person, but sometimes I think my humility was too extreme and it ultimately worked against me. I didn't want to speak highly of myself for fear that it would bring someone else down. Now I speak highly of myself when I know it is warranted, because it's not about bringing someone else down, but it's about being a beacon of light that others can aspire to.

In order to push myself forward, I think about the potential outcome if I do push myself versus if I don't. At the end of the day, I strive to be better so I can help others achieve their goals, whether it's on a personal level or at a corporate level.

I see myself as someone who is always on a quest to better herself and to go further than she's gone before, mentally, spiritually and materially. Honestly, I don't dwell on how others see me. But others have told me that they view me as an honest and upright individual.

I work on self-acceptance by changing things that are in my ability to change and praying about the things that I cannot. What I value most in my life is my relationship with God, my health, my family and friends, and happiness in what I do with my time.

Beautiful, I feel that your biggest struggles are self-image issues, acceptance issues, and the need to feel loved. A weak family foundation may contribute to your struggle, as well as unsupportive parents and friends. Also, it might be that you don't have a family or network that doesn't pray and accept you for who you are, and no one is committed to mentoring you.

If I had the opportunity to sit with a young girl who is a shadow of my younger self, I would tell her, "Faith can move mountains. If you believe you can do it, see yourself doing it, and speak it over yourself. Over time, your mind will start to believe it and it will happen."

- Cheryl

Dear Beautiful,

My name is Abigail and I am in my 40s. I was born in Haiti and I live in the United States.

When I was growing up, I wanted to be an engineer at NASA. Today, I am a civil engineer. I would like to think that the special gift I have been blessed with is the ability to listen.

I am very passionate about helping others succeed, and when I am doing that, I feel invigorated. If I could not do that, I would feel like I am not fulfilling my purpose in life.

As a child, the thing I feared most was not being successful enough at school. As a teenager, I feared not finding the right partner for a brighter future. As a young woman, I feared for the future of my children. Now, in this current space, I feel at peace since I know my future is not in my hands.

If I could go back and speak to my younger self, I would tell her to continue to dream big! The more you believe in yourself, the more others will too.

My biggest challenges have been managing work, home and all aspects of life. To help me combat those challenges, I am applying balance and delegating as much as possible. I also empower others and don't try to be perfect all the time. When things get difficult in my life, I seek spiritual help from God.

I feel that I hold myself back sometimes in that I do not want to embrace success because it is a step you cannot back away from. Once you have reached that level, you have to give up privacy and learn to live behind the podium. However, in order to push myself forward, I tell myself that success does not always equate to being out in the open and giving up my privacy.

I see myself as a great and accomplished woman, and I feel that others see me similarly. In order to work on self-acceptance, I first think about the fact that my flaws are what make me unique. What I value most in life is my relationship with my God.

Beautiful, I think that your biggest struggles have to do with your moral compass and how you see yourself compared to what's happening in certain industries, especially the modeling world. I think what contributes to those struggles are the mixed signals from the entertainment business.

If I had the opportunity to sit with a young girl who is a shadow of my younger self, I would tell her, "You had better have some dreams, and please let them be big. The bigger the dreams, the more they have a chance of materializing. Once one of them has been fruitful, find another one quickly, because if you rehash your past accomplishments, it is because you are not doing anything of significance today."

- *Abigail*

Dear Beautiful,

My name is Luciana and I am in my 30s. I was born in Brazil and I live in the United States.

When I was growing up, I wanted to be many things – a lawyer, a doctor, a jockey. But I never stopped wanting to become a history professor. I wanted to go to Greece, Italy, Egypt, Turkey and dig up old neighborhoods, find treasures, and touch something that belonged to someone 3,000 years ago, who had the same problems and dreams that I have today. I also just wanted an Indiana Jones hat - I still want his hat!

Today, I am a User Experience Researcher. I make websites and apps user friendly by examining how people find their way through a website or app. I'm a tech geek, and I love it. I still have a burning love for the ancient world, but the possibilities of where technology can go in the future has its own type of enchantment. I personally love the moments in my life when I can find a connection between the technology of today and the technology of the past. Just the other day, I found an old wax tablet that I have – a replica of what Romans used to write on. It's just a thin piece of wood with a coating of wax that you can write on with a metal stylus. Well today, I run usability tests on iPads-which are tablets you can write on with a stylus.

I think when it comes to gifts, I am blessed with curiosity. It keeps me interested in this world, even when things turn dark out there. There is always something to discover, to learn, to wonder about. The invention of the internet is by far the greatest thing to have ever happened to me. So much information is available in a matter of seconds. I never feel bored.

I am passionate about ideas. I would love to work for a think tank for people. I participated in something like this in Washington D.C - it was called House of Genius. People came to us (a group of 20 tech individuals) with their ideas for a new business venture. We would hear their presentation, and then provide feedback and ideas on how to make their business idea stronger.

When I'm doing the things I am passionate about, I feel like that passion loves you back. Like it knows who you are, and syncs so easily and effortlessly with you – like a soul mate. The hours pass like seconds. But only a few people are lucky enough to have found and practice that love every day. Most people have to say goodbye to that soul mate, and go home to the one they settled with.

If I were not able to do those things, like I feel nowadays – I suppose I would feel a little depressed. By depressed, I mean restrained. While I enjoy my job, it still feels like a job - a task I do in exchange for money. When you spend most of your time exchanging your energy for money – you can't help but feel a little depressed or "pressed down".

Unfortunately, what I feared most as a child, teenager, and young woman – continues to this day. I don't feel good enough. I am not sure if I don't feel good enough for society's multitude of standards (especially for women), or if I don't feel good enough for my own standards. At times, I find society's standards easier to meet than my own standards for myself. Regardless, it's exhausting.

Regarding those fears in present day life, oh, it's still there. When it's really bad, I practice a Buddhist technique I learned. I invite those feelings to sit with me, I give it the time to speak, to tell me what the problem is. Then I simply say: "thank you, but I am going to do it anyway." It doesn't always immediately work – but sometimes the fight alone is all you need for your own voice to silence the noise.

If you could go back and speak to my younger self, I would tell her to move to California. I was accepted to the University of San Francisco to study graphic design in my early 20s. My life could have been filled with sunshine, hipsters, authenticity, and art. But I was terrified of going alone, and terrified of the cost, so I didn't go. Ironically, I would up with a much larger student loan debt. Skipping out on California remains my biggest regret. I feel that the east coast created a colder me - someone who is smart and capable, sure, but also someone with solid walls she likes to pretend is resilience.

As a woman, I feel like one of my biggest challenges is – being a woman. Sit with that statement for a while. Any woman at any age in any location in this world can feel the weight of that statement. It has never been about one challenge, or the biggest challenge. It has always been a series of bloody battles raging on the outside and on the inside.

To combat those challenges, I surround myself with strong women. For example, I am extremely picky about my small circle of friends. My friends are resilient, intelligent, caring, creative, hard-working, honest, and introspective. Most of all – my friends are fighters. They understand that being a woman is difficult, that our decisions are difficult, and they march on anyway. I don't have close male friends. I haven't (yet) been able to find a man with the same range of emotional maturity (sorry guys) as my female friends have. Often-times challenges are not new. Someone, somewhere experienced them. Find people whom you know handled those challenges with poise, a good fight, maybe even a little grace – and surround yourself with those type of people.

When things get difficult and I need help, I call on myself first. At 37 years of age, I feel that if I am old enough to give advice to someone, I am old enough to give advice to myself. However, I am always open to external guidance, so if a problem is particularly difficult I find the right person to help me explore solutions, or at least explore acceptance.

The way in which I believe I hold myself back is that I am an over-thinker. I often talk myself out of my own good ideas because I am afraid of failure. The sad thing is that you automatically fail at anything that you don't try – so I am fully aware of how circular this mindset is.

I do find ways to push myself forward and I do that by taking calculated risks, but I take risks now. Last year, I quit my job without another one lined up. I fell in love with someone, and I wanted to move near them. I gave up an apartment I loved, and left friends and family behind to be near this person. Every cell in my body screamed at me not to do it, because there is nothing more unpredictable than romantic relationships. But there was this little voice in my head telling me: "well, what if?" I obeyed it. One month after I moved into that new city, we broke up. I was devastated, and furious. But being alone in a new city forced me to examine my life. I can't say yet what doors have opened for me, but I can feel that doors did open. Something in me changed, and that change is good.

I see myself as a work in constant progress. I am in many ways my best friend and my own worst enemy. I demand a lot from myself, but when I achieve something, I am my loudest cheerleader.

So how do others see me? Let's see…I am often called a curmudgeon, or an old white man. I actually take this as a compliment because if I am an old white man – that means I made it. The United States congress is not made up of bubbly cheerleaders – just sayin'… But all joking aside, this is a hard question to answer. What we feel inside projects to the outside. We have tainted lenses that we use to experience the world. So in a way, I think my friends are right. I am that archaic man who is impatient and unforgiving of mistakes - because I often do not forgive myself. However, I am also the one that many of my friends come to for honest (sometimes brutal) advice when they need it the most.

The way I've worked on self-acceptance is by not wanting to be Jesus. I am not very religious, but I came from a religious family. At 15 years of age I decided to leave the church my family belongs to. This happened because of a particularly strange day. I was sitting in class, surrounded by soon-to-be devout teenagers, when the teacher asked us who we wanted to be like. The whole class (minus me) exclaimed: "Jeeeeeeesuuuuuus," in that cult-like rhythm you only see in 80s movies. I remember thinking: "Why? The dude died horribly…" The thing is, Jesus had his path, his purpose, his story – it was his and his alone. We can admire someone, sure, but we need to live our own truth – our own story.

What I value most in my own life is freedom. That privilege of being. That privilege of having access to the word no, or the word yes. The privilege of designing my life, and of making my own mistakes.

The biggest struggle for girls today is being a girl in the age of social media. When we hear about celebrity teenagers breaking down and rebelling or sometimes dying – we often blame it all on the pressures of a childhood spent in the public eye. This used to happen only to celebrity kids. Now, it's an epidemic, and it's all because of social media robbing children of their childhood. I am on the end tail of the millennium generation. The internet came out in full force when I was in middle school. I can look back in time and find a childhood that was hard at times, but survivable, and at times utterly happy.

I feel that girls today have no context of what childhood used to be like. All they know is a world where a stranger's acceptance or "like" is more important than their own. A world where parents who are supposed to parent you, are instead having affairs in the same social media venues their kids are using. A world where a girl may be wanting to end her life, but instead has to post happy pictures – because "no one likes a grump." A world where a girl can get raped, and it ends up going viral. How can you find yourself amidst all that noise?

In contemplating what may contribute to these struggles, okay, old white man talk time. Let me get my cane… Republicans have an obsession with gay marriage. They blame gays for the dismantling of marriage, for the degeneration of youth, for the color fuchsia. The truth is, so much of this "breakdown of society" is because of isolation. We feel alone. We feel that the world is quite literally on our shoulders. Survival of the fittest has become the law of the land, and we have forgotten that in order to grow within, we have to first find ourselves through true connection with others. Social Media, to me, is a symptom of extreme isolation. We are clumsily looking for fast connection, any connection, because we forgot how to build strong friendships, romances, and partnerships through work and time. No satisfying, fulfilling human connection can be built with a tweet.

When it's all said and done, if you can all imagine for a moment that I am sitting with a young girl who is a shadow of my younger self, would I have anything to say to her about dreams? No. I would ask her to tell me about dreams. No adult should tell a child about dreams. We don't know what that means anymore.

- Luciana

FLIGHT 9: FLIGHT PLAN

For each person that has chosen to read this book, I hope that it has inspired you to think of your flight plan. We all want to grow and fly and reach heights higher than our predecessors, higher than what our forefathers hoped for us. If only we could see that the hope for bigger dreams is within us—and only us—then we would know that taking flight is a matter of taking life one day at a time and breaking down each dream into a smaller piece, so that when we are ready, we won't just dream of flying, but flying high to a self - undiscovered, to success untapped, and to the best dreams we can ourselves dream.

Please answer the questions that the women in this book have all answered and make sure you keep it close to your heart. Or better yet, write it to someone who is in need of a letter to help keep their dreams alive.

When I was growing up, I wanted to be _____

Today, I am a/an:

_____ (If you
are a working professional)

Do you feel like you have special gifts? If so, what are they?

_____

_____

_____

_____

What are you passionate about now?

_____

_____

_____

_____

How do you feel when you are doing the things you are passionate
about?

_____

_____

_____

_____

If you could not do the things you are passionate about, how would you feel?

_____

_____

_____

_____

What did you fear most as a child, a teenager, and a young woman?

_____

_____

_____

_____

How do you feel about those fears now?

_____

_____

_____

_____

If you could go back and speak to your younger self, what would you say to her?

_____

_____

_____

_____

As a woman, what do you feel has been one of your biggest challenges?

_____

_____

_____

_____

What do you do to combat those challenges?

_____

_____

_____

_____

Who do you seek help from when things get difficult?

_____

_____

_____

_____

In what ways do you feel you hold yourself back?

_____

_____

_____

_____

What are some of the things you do to help push yourself forward?

_____

_____

_____

_____

How do you see yourself?

_____

_____

_____

_____

How do feel like others see you?

_____

_____

_____

_____

How do you work on self-acceptance?

_____

_____

_____

_____

What do you value most in your own life?

_____

_____

_____

_____

For young girls today, what do you feel their biggest struggles are?

_____

_____

_____

_____

What do you think contribute to those struggles?

_____

_____

_____

_____

If you had the opportunity to sit with a young girl who is a shadow of your younger self, what might you say to her about dreams?

_____

_____

_____

_____

FLIGHT 10: RESOURCES

As I began reading the responses that each of these women had so unselfishly given, I couldn't help but think of their bravery. They were willing to share their own personal stories of triumph, courage, bravery, heartbreak, difficult circumstances, challenges, past hurts, and abuse in different forms. I immediately felt the awesomeness of the responsibility I had to tell their stories honestly and with care.

Sharing my own thoughts, insights and letter was in many ways cathartic for me. I touched on some issues that have affected me, including depression. A large amount of women are willing to suffer silently, as I did for many years, but I hope that I can spread the word that help is available. In 2000, I first sought help from a professional to help me sort through my issues. Mental health issues have been kept undercover for too long; there is such a stigma that still exists for those who suffer. Though some seek out help, too many are still suffering silently.

In sharing these letters, it was also my hope that if someone were to identify with one or more of these women, they would know that there is light at the end of the tunnel, and sometimes in the middle of it. The women in this book range in age from 20s to 80s, and that selection was purposeful.

I believe that prayer and meditation are an important part of healing and feeling positive about the things that afflict us, but I also want to let everyone reading this know that help is available in many forms for those who seek it. So with this in mind, I have included a few organizations and groups that you can seek help from to deal with issues that perhaps friends and family members are not equipped to help you with. There are numerous others available online.

We are not all born with the tools to help each other. The best healing I think we can provide for each other is support and love. In making this book the movement that I want to create, I will offer more resources for help via social media, so please be aware of those as well. This is where communication comes full circle, and this is where offering help becomes universal, because with every person we help at whatever age, background, color or creed, we are indeed able to bridge the divide, love even more deeply, and fly even higher. We might even soar!

Women's Resource Center to Help Domestic Violence
https://www.wrcdv.org/

National Suicide Prevention Lifeline
http://suicidepreventionlifeline.org/

Women in Crisis Shelter – The Family Tree
http://www.thefamilytree.org/en/domestic-violence-services/106

Employee Assistance from your employer – Many companies provide this assistance for their employees, and the details of your participation remain confidential.

Licensed Therapists and Psychology Professionals – With the assistance of primary care practices, you can receive names of local professionals who will be able to treat you if you are suffering from any of the issues we sometimes deal with.

Stay connected on Instagram and Twitter at the handle **@letters4flying**

Regardless of the circumstances we all face, regardless of how hard we feel we must fight, we are all each other's keepers and we are all part of a beautiful collaboration. We are each individually beautiful and a **GIFT – Girls In Flight Team!**

ABOUT THE AUTHOR

Shona Bramble is a communications professional who has worked in the industry for over 20 years in various capacities. She is of West-Indian heritage – being born in the Eastern Caribbean island of St. Vincent and the Grenadines. She migrated to the United States in 1988 and has lived in the Washington, D.C. area ever since. Shona earned a Master's Degree in Information Technology Management and an MBA at the University of Maryland, University College. She is a communicator at heart and expresses her love of it through her writing, poetry and photography. She is also a mentor in public speaking, which has allowed her to help others in finding their voice.

43723101R00065

Made in the USA
Middletown, DE
17 May 2017